Shakespeare
A Teaching Guide

Sharon Hamilton

J. Weston Walch, Publisher
Portland, Maine

On the cover: William Shakespeare, attrib. to John Taylor
by courtesy of the National Portrait Gallery, London

1   2   3   4   5   6   7   8   9   10

ISBN 0-8251-2157-4

For my father

Contents

Annotated Table of Contents

Introduction

Chapter 1. Shakespeare Anxiety

Introduction to my interest in Shakespeare and to these techniques.

Understanding the Text: Discussing, Responding, Acting

Chapter 2. The Cast List and Opening Episodes: Hamlet

A ready way into the text is to have the class read the cast list out loud, pausing to discuss each seemingly related group of characters. This exercise helps students to become familiar with the strange-sounding names, and to note relationships, ranks, and potential conflicts. A second technique is to do dramatic readings of the opening episodes, stopping at the introduction of each new character to discuss what the episode accomplishes.

Chapter 3. The Quiz Revisited: Hamlet

This chapter presents six brief questions on Act I of *Hamlet*, designed to test not merely fact but also understanding—of motive, language, and event. The chapter also describes the process of designing a quiz and its goal of putting the teacher in the position of new reader.

Chapter 4. Mime as Meaning: Hamlet

This chapter describes two pantomime exercises that bring out the subtext—the understanding of character that some students might feel but have trouble expressing in words. The first asks everyone to mime a particular emotion that one of the characters is feeling—e.g., for Hamlet, depression; for Marcellus, terror; for Claudius, triumph. The second, more complex exercise asks volunteers to pair up and mime opposite sides of Claudius's nature: his public and private faces.

Chapter 5. *The Live Sculpture:* Hamlet

This is a more complex mime exercise, in which the student "sculptor" casts classmates and then arranges them in a group sculpture of some key moment in an act—e.g., the balcony scene in *Romeo and Juliet*, Oswald's attack on the blind Gloucester in *King Lear*, or Claudius's first public audience in *Hamlet*. The rest of the class serves as audience and, when the arrangement is complete, as commentators on these silent scenes.

Chapter 6. *Speaking the Speech: The Sonnet and the Dramatic Monologue—* Antony and Cleopatra

Each student memorizes and presents to the class a brief passage—sonnet, soliloquy, or monologue. Performing a speech gives students a stake in understanding each word—you can't say convincingly what you don't understand—as well as a chance to occupy the spotlight.

Chapter 7. *Acting the Short Episode:* Othello *and* The Taming of the Shrew

This chapter describes the acting of short (20–40 lines) episodes, cast by the teacher and memorized, blocked, and presented by the students.

Writing About Shakespeare: Five Kinds of Papers

Chapter 8. *The Critical Essay:* Hamlet

This is a description of several prewriting techniques for discovering a thesis and beginning a rough draft. First, the teacher offers a list of suggested topics, organized by category. Next, the student chooses a topic, brainstorms, and devises a thesis statement. Then the student presents a draft of the statement for the rest of the class to critique. The chapter describes several kinds of faulty thesis statements, as well as means of strengthening them. Next, the student learns how to break the writing process into stages, to separate the stage of generating ideas from the stages of organizing and expressing them. The first of these stages, also described in the chapter, is a conference with the teacher on a short section of the rough draft.

Chapter 9. The Invented Diary: Othello, Macbeth, and The Taming of the Shrew

This is a paper written in the voice and from the point of view of a key character—e.g., Edmund from *King Lear* or Kate from *The Taming of the Shrew*. It lets the student describe moments that take place offstage and supply motives and thoughts for characters who do not confide everything to the audience.

Chapter 10. The Parody: King Lear

Like the diary, this is a chance for the student to look at the play from a new angle, this time the oblique one of Monty Pythonesque whimsy. Through exaggeration or understatement, it takes a different view of the original and yet is entertaining in its own right.

Chapter 11. Director's Choices: Branagh's Henry V

This is a critique of a scene from a videotape, based on the choices that the director has made in casting, lighting, costuming, blocking, setting, and editing. It is an exercise in comparison—written after students have read the play, seen the rest of the videotape and, if possible, compared it with another performance.

Chapter 12. The Student as Director: Antony and Cleopatra

This assignment asks the student to describe how she or he would direct a key episode from a play that the class has studied. It may be a scene that is not staged in the original, such as the opening or closing moments, before the first line of dialogue or after the last. Or it may be a climactic moment—a duel, a proposal, a trial. As with the critique of the videotape (Chapter 11), a key aim is for students to realize that there is no one "correct" interpretation of the play, that in every production, including their own, the director must make crucial choices.

A Bit of Background

Chapter 13. Shakespeare's Language

This chapter describes the barriers to understanding that Shakespeare's language can present. It concentrates on students' puzzlement over the concept of blank verse and provides exercises for helping them understand the uses that Shakespeare made of dramatic poetry.

Chapter 14. Shakespeare's Theater

This chapter describes Shakespeare's Globe Theater in its heyday by means of an imaginary visit. It follows Rafe, a shoemaker's apprentice, as he steals away from an afternoon's work for his first trip to the Bankside.

Chapter 1

Shakespeare Anxiety

Why another book on Shakespeare? The answer was implied in the comic strip *Crock* a few years back. The fat harem girl is flirting with a member of the Lost Patrol. "How do you feel about me, Maggot?" she prompts. "You ain't too awful bad," he manages to say at last. "It ain't Shakespeare," she beams, "but I'll take it." If it were Shakespeare, she implies, Maggot's response would be poetry: Just the name represents the standard of eloquence and culture. But a lot of people lack her rotund complacency. Shakespeare seems to them up there in the airy reaches with ancient Greek and calculus—abstruse, scary, and boring.

It *is* hard not to be wary of Shakespeare, or at least of his reputation. The great name is evoked constantly in political speeches, novels, even TV sitcoms. The plays have been a mainstay of theater companies for 400 years. In any given week, some group, amateur or professional, in New York or London or Tokyo or Bucharest, is sure to be staging something by Shakespeare. The leading roles—Hamlet, Cleopatra, Shylock, Rosalind—remain the most coveted in the repertory, the pinnacle of an actor's career. A new film of one of the plays, such as Kenneth Branagh's *Henry V* or Franco Zeffirelli's *Hamlet*, can be both a classic interpretation and a hit. Not only is Shakespeare famous; he is the most famous author in the world.

Not surprisingly, Shakespeare continues to be the author most frequently taught in American high schools. That fact is not always greeted with enthusiasm by our students. Even those of us who love reading and seeing the plays may be susceptible to Shakespeare anxiety when we're asked to teach them. A major cause of this anxiety is that most of us have been given so little guidance about how to go about it. The college lecture model doesn't work with squirming high school sophomores: Talked at, they tend to tune out, like the glazed-over class in *Ferris Bueller's Day Off*. Nor is the large body of criticism much help: While the scholars are pondering a possible medieval analogue for *The Merchant of Venice* or the Folio lineation of a scene, students are trying to distinguish Antonio from Bassanio and wondering whether "blank verse" isn't just a fancy name for prose. We teachers are left with the Prufrockian quandaries: "So how should I presume? And how shall I begin?"

Shakespeare: A Teaching Guide is meant to answer both questions. It describes techniques for reading and writing about Shakespeare that have evolved in my own classes. I have taught on several levels, from ninth grade through graduate school, and to students with a wide range of sensibilities—jocks and poets, remedial readers and National Merit finalists, underachievers and perfectionists. Shakespeare, I have found, can appeal to them all—but not in the same ways or through the same means. This book recounts what my own teachers and students have taught me about how Shakespeare can speak to us.

I know from personal experience that Shakespeare can be taught well in high school. In the eleventh grade, at a public school in Detroit, I was introduced to *Macbeth*, and to his creator, by a master teacher, Leo Cierpial, Ph.D., aesthete, lover of words and ideas. He made us see that the witches are both eerie and entrancing, the Macbeths repellent and vulnerable, the verse melodic and understandable. He took the play seriously, but he was confident enough of its greatness to treat it playfully. One day the class rebel challenged the claim that Shakespeare wrote in blank verse. He refused to believe that the lines had a regular rhythm, that they were anything more than oddly spaced prose, that any playwright could sustain iambic pentameter for five acts. Dr. C. replied coolly, "Oh, it's just a question of practice. The meter acts like a metronome—get it going in your head and out come the words in the right rhythm." And he launched into a spontaneous parody of the dagger soliloquy, turning it into a cigarette ad: "Is this a Camel I see before me, the filter toward my face?/Come, let me puff thee. I have thee not and yet I taste thee still."

I laughed in sudden understanding. The strange rhythms of the lines had enchanted me from the first scenes. Long before I could understand what the Macbeths were inflicting on others or suffering themselves, I simply enjoyed the sounds of the words. At sixteen, my memory was quick and supple. The weird sisters' spells entered into it effortlessly. Dr. Cierpial's requirement that we memorize one of the long passages made me hear Macbeth's voice. The "tomorrow and tomorrow" soliloquy touched my imagination—made me see the dusty passage, the flickering candle, the bellowing idiot. It was a revelation to imagine Shakespeare himself tapping out the lines—and to realize that making fun of them did not diminish their intrinsic worth.

The following year, the same teacher taught me *Hamlet*. Almost from the prince's first appearance, I was smitten. He sounded so bright and funny and unhappy—more fascinating and more screwed up than my brightest and most neurotic friends. I read my favorite scenes over and over. The week we finished studying the play, Olivier's *Hamlet* happened to be on television. I do not come from a family of readers, much less Shakespeare fans. When I told my dad that *Hamlet* was playing, he said, "Yeah? Third base or shortstop?" The night of the broadcast, he was off bowling and the younger kids were asleep. I tried to explain the plot to my mother, who had gamely joined me. But after a few polite "Oh, really" 's she dozed off, too.

I sat in front of the flickering screen, transfixed by Olivier's resonant voice, Jean Simmons's delicate prettiness, the bleak, magnificent castle. Even Sir Laurence's chopped-off bleach job and the bathtub sailboat staging of the pirates' attack could not spoil the illusion. I was furious at Ophelia. How could she be such a Daddy's girl? Didn't she know that Hamlet needed her? It was like the fantasy I'd had at ten, before I learned that girls couldn't become major league baseball players: the Detroit Tigers were down two runs in the bottom of the ninth and the manager gave me the nod to pinch hit—move over, Ophie, I'm coming into that play! That's the feeling, I realized later, that moved some people to become actors and others to write plays of their own. On the screen, Hamlet gave his thrilling war cry and leapt onto the cringing Claudius. Then came the rapid series of deaths, the farewell in Horatio's arms, the solemn death march, with the prince's head dangling like a broken doll's. Face burning, I shook my mother awake—it was 1:00 A.M. by then—and tried to describe in a tumble of hyperboles this actor, this play, this playwright.

Many syllabi and term papers and final exams later, I discovered that loving Shakespeare is very different from teaching him. It can even be a detriment. Teachers tend to teach best those students who are younger versions of themselves, whose tastes and learning styles resemble their own. Words, written and spoken, come easily to me. When I first began to teach, I approached Shakespeare's plays as though they were novels that happened to be written in dialogue. We read and discussed them, and then my students wrote essays on the recurrent metaphors or the role of a foil character or the importance of a particular scene—all the sanctioned literary topics that I had written on myself. Some students, whose minds worked like mine, proved articulate, even eloquent critics. Since then, I have discovered more ways to help them devise clear, imaginative essays.

But literary criticism is a specialized genre. When it is forced on a writer, it can kill confidence and interest. Too many of the essays were thin or prosaic or dead in the middle, written in Englishpaperese by people who only half understood the play and the topic. They were bored by their papers—and so was I. Something was missing from discussions, too, especially as we went on with a play. Some students were just going through the motions or were silent and disaffected. Too much of the energy, I sensed, was coming from me. I felt frustrated by people who could not grasp a scene simply by reading it or express their thoughts in a well-reasoned essay, and offended by some who found Shakespeare boring.

I see now that the basic problem was that my student model was wrong—I was trying to turn all of them into novice scholars. Most high school students are not potential college professors or literary critics or even English majors. In the future, most are more likely to encounter Shakespeare—if at all—in performance than on the page. Most are more likely to read Shakespeare in high school than in college. While Shakespeare's work remains a staple of the high school curriculum, in college these days only traditional literature majors are expected to study him. For the rest, the elimination of core requirements and survey courses, the tendency to specialize early, and the controversy about "the canon" often set a Shakespeareless course. I eventually realized that for many of my students I would be providing not only their first but also their only experience of studying Shakespeare.

Blaming them for what was going wrong with the class got me nowhere. I began rethinking my own experience of learning Shakespeare. What wasn't I doing? I wasn't having my students memorize passages or see productions. I added those components, and it helped. But some people found the memorization excruciating or the performances affected, and both took a lot of class time. I began visiting colleagues' classes, to see how they taught Shakespeare. In one, Mr. Y, a veteran teacher, was having ninth graders read all of *The Merchant of Venice* out loud. Students read in turn—no one had to be Shylock for a whole scene—and they were encouraged to interrupt for questions and comments. But almost no one did—except the teacher. The reading went on, and all sense of emphasis and of individual voice got lost in the drone. It took eight or nine weeks to get through the play; homework was devoted to outside reading of a long novel, so no time was lost, he assured me uneasily. But in this reverence for every word of Shakespeare, the readers got so entangled in the branches of arcane syntax and convoluted vocabulary that they could not stand back and see individual trees, much less the forest. And no one was having much fun.

In another class, Ms. X, a new teacher, took the opposite approach. She asked a group of seniors to read *Hamlet* for the next day. They, and I, trooped into class red-eyed and yawning. "Okay," she said, "take out a sheet of paper. Now summarize the plot in twenty-five words or less." We gasped, swallowed, and got to work. The exercise taught us that the plot is complicated and melodramatic, and that everything centers on the prince. It also emphasized the value of terseness. And it was fun, like every good word game. We read each other our summaries and cheered for people who fit in the key events and stayed within the word limit. That process took about half an hour. Ms. X then gave a panicky glance at the clock and asked lamely, "Uhhh…so what did you think of Polonius?" After class, she turned to me: "What am I going to do for the next three weeks?" Her approach had the focus and the liveliness that Mr. Y's lacked, but it was too narrow and too superficial. It suggested that the most important element in *Hamlet* is the plot, and it left students to cope on their own with the intricacies of language and character. As Ms. X sensed, having "covered" the play once, her students were not likely to reread it with much enthusiasm.

Now I call those methods the long and the short of it. They, too, I realized, were variations on the "novice scholar" model. They failed to tap other talents that many students brought to class: an intuitive understanding of people, athletic grace and energy, spatial orientation, a sense of humor. I know now that many actors and directors, including great ones, are better at showing their understanding of a play than at explaining it. I sensed that getting students on their feet is the surest way of getting them into the text.

But how to adapt that insight to my classes? I thought that my goal had to be a polished, full-scale production—that my students had to become junior Oliviers and Redgraves. Acting, done "right," takes more space and much more time than I had available in an English class, I rationalized. Besides, I had other books on the syllabus to cover. I'd just leave the acting to the drama department. Secretly, I was terrified at the prospect of stepping into the unfamiliar role of director, and possibly making a fool of myself in front of my entire class. The old methods worked for some students, I kept telling myself, even while admitting that some of my liveliest classes grew out of spontaneous dramatic readings of a scene or discussions of how a set might be designed.

The breakthrough came with support from the National Endowment for the Humanities, which allowed me to study with such scholars as Miriam Gilbert, Robert Smallwood, and Russell Jackson, and to attend workshops by directors and actors from the Royal Shakespeare Company and Tina Packer's Shakespeare & Company. Those teachers freed me to try what I sensed my students needed. This book takes its inspiration from their practical knowledge and enthusiasm.

It is not that I have discarded everything I used to do. I still stress reading and discussing and writing about Shakespeare. I still try to help students appreciate subtleties of language and complexities of character, to recognize patterns and techniques unique to plays and unique to Shakespeare, to develop a vocabulary of terms that allows a clearer understanding not only of the play at hand but also of any future Shakespeare they see or read. But I have modified and varied my methods to build my students' confidence as well as their knowledge. That means resisting the stance of the expert: not lecturing, but creating a class dialogue in which I, too, am a learner. All plays, including Shakespeare's, are about people, after all, and some of my least intellectual students are the most astute judges of character. My approach, therefore, appeals to my students' visual and aural as well as verbal intelligence. Above all, I want to give my students access to the plays, to make them theirs—not the critics', not the actors', not mine.

Now I want to share my experiences with other teachers. *Shakespeare: A Teaching Guide* is written in the belief that the best way to teach teachers is to invite them into your own classroom and let them watch you work. This book deals with some basic questions: What is there to say about a play by Shakespeare? How can readers be helped to distinguish between the characters' voices—to "hear" differences in tone, social status, and motivation? How can we assure that assignments are taken seriously and yet keep the play in the play?

My methods are presented in roughly the order in which you might want to use them, beginning with ways of introducing a play and ending with variations on the final paper. The techniques are illustrated by descriptions and writing samples from my students' work over the past several years. For the sake of unity, the early chapters concentrate on Shakespeare's most frequently taught play, *Hamlet*, taking you through several means of approaching Act I. The next chapters describe techniques to use later in the teaching process, focusing on a different play for each technique. Altogether, there are fourteen chapters, including this introduction. Chapters 2 through 7 describe techniques designed for the classroom—discussions, quizzes, and acting exercises, with suggestions for adapting them to students of various age and ability levels, from junior high to adult. Chapters 8 through 12, intended for students from eighth grade up, cover writing assignments, including four alternatives to the traditional critical essay. The book ends with two brief chapters on Shakespeare's language and theater. A more detailed, annotated table of contents precedes this introduction.

These are not radical techniques, not means for jazzing up or getting around the plays. My basic approach is the traditional one of active reading: helping students cope with Shakespeare's diction and methods and then making them responsible for their own learning. The techniques are not meant to be exclusive. Although each chapter applies a method to a particular play, the method could be adapted to any of Shakespeare's works. Nor are these approaches intended to be inclusive: They should certainly not all be used with the same play or even during the same semester. I would expect many readers of *Shakespeare: A Teaching Guide* to read *in* it rather than through it—to concentrate on the chapters that discuss a technique or a play that interests them. The choices would depend on the time and resources of the teacher and the nature of the class.

My teaching model is the theater itself. Theater is a communal experience. Actors, amateur and professional, have said that they can sense an audience's mood and that they take energy from a responsive group. On a smaller scale, teachers also take inspiration from their audiences. Whether the hearer is a student, a conference participant, or the reader of a book like this one, the pleasure increases when the experience is shared. The sharing is not always public or immediate. It may come in solitude, sometimes long after the initial encounter. We seldom know the long-term effects of our teaching—or even the shape that our ideas take in other minds. This book will have served its purpose if it gives to other teachers and students some new access to Shakespeare's infinite variety.

Chapter 2

The Cast List and Opening Episodes: *Hamlet*

The Cast List

Once I asked a class nervously anticipating their first assignment to write down, in a sentence or two, what they had heard about *Hamlet*. Some responses were silly: "It's about this guy in black tights who carries a skull around with him." Others were earnest: "It's a tragedy. I think Hamlet is a prince." "Isn't this the play with 'to be or not to be' in it?" Some were wary: "*Hamlet* is a play by Shakespeare which is difficult to read." One student said outright that it would be "boring," and another wrote, with mock modesty, that the play "is very well known by many people except myself." Through the comments ran a strain of awe tinged with either rebellion or fear. We did not read them aloud in class—people were feeling self-conscious enough already. We put them away till after we had finished the play. Then students could laugh at their own expectations.

They probably did not guess that I was feeling similar qualms. I had taught the play only once before, with limited success. I was going to begin with a quiz on Act I, the assigned reading for the day. Before I could ask the first question, Joe Parziale waved his hand. "Wait, wait. Why doesn't this Claudius guy want O—O—What's her name—to see Hamlet any more?"

"What? Claudius isn't involved in that decision."

"He's not? He's her dad, isn't he?"

"Check the names, Joe. Claudius is the *king*."

"Well, how can I keep these guys straight? The names all sound alike—and they're all hard."

"Can someone help Joe out?"

7

"Look at the first page. There's a list of the characters."

"Yeah—where? I missed that."

"Maybe we should go over the cast list before we do the quiz."

A collective sigh of relief greeted that suggestion. Now I always begin the first Shakespeare play of the semester by asking students to turn to the cast list. Even if they have started reading the play on their own, many, like Joe before them, will have skipped the list and plunged into the opening scene with only a dim idea of who is talking to whom. Shakespeare's own audience often knew the plot before they entered the theater. And they had the benefit of watching a full performance, with signals about characters' relationships and motives in the costumes, accents, and movements. We have to gather such information from mere words on the page, and not even words in our own idiom. On the other hand, we have the advantage of being able to read—to go through a play at our own pace and to reconsider words that puzzle us the first time through.

The cast list can serve as an entree to everything from how names are pronounced to what possible conflicts might arise. The technique works like this: I ask someone to begin reading the dramatis personae aloud, stopping the first time she thinks she has come to the end of a whole group of characters. At each pause, the reader and then her classmates comment or ask questions. If necessary, I prod or summarize. The first entry is "Claudius, King of Denmark." He seems to be in a category by himself. What can we surmise from his name and title? For one thing, that the play is about the nobility. The first character listed is the king, and a scan of the rest of the cast shows that it contains princes and "courtiers" and their servants. What is a courtier? Someone who serves at the king's *court*. So one way of identifying a character is by profession: Voltemand, Cornelius, Rosencrantz, and Guildenstern— what long names!—are Claudius's courtiers. Why is Claudius listed first? Isn't Hamlet the main character? Yes, but Claudius has the highest rank. So rank is one way of categorizing people.

After the discussion of Claudius, I call on a new reader. As "Prince of Denmark," Hamlet is listed next, and "Polonius, Lord Chamberlain" third. What's a lord chamberlain? A sort of high cabinet officer, like our secretary of state. Wait a minute; Hamlet is "son to the late, and nephew to the present King." Why isn't Hamlet king now instead of his uncle? Aha, the plot thickens.

By now, students will have begun to look ahead. I often vary the sequence of the list in order to answer questions or to make connections. For example, at this point someone may notice other signs of trouble: One of the characters is the "Ghost of Hamlet's Father," and two others are "gravediggers." This does not sound like a comedy. But the gravediggers are also called "Clowns." Are they in the play to lighten the tone, like the servants in *Romeo and Juliet*? What is that called? Oh yeah, comic relief. I might add that "clown" can also mean "country bumpkin"—hayseed. When we read the play, I say, we'll see which of those meanings applies.

What other kinds of information can we get from the list? The setting: it's "Elsinore." Wait, isn't Claudius the king of *Denmark*? Oh, Elsinore is his castle. But why is the play set in Denmark? Wasn't Shakespeare English? Do the names seem to have a Danish ring? No— "Claudius" and "Polonius" sound Roman; "Rosencrantz and Guildenstern," German; "Reynaldo" and "Ophelia," Italian. How Danish is Hamlet's world? Did Shakespeare know anything firsthand about Denmark? If not, why did he set this play there? Let's save those questions, too, for later on. Other points? There's also a "Prince of Norway" and "a Norwegian Captain." What are the Norwegian characters doing in here? The Norwegian prince's name is Fortinbras—"strong in arms." Is there going to be a war between the two countries?

Look—the only two female characters, "Gertrude, Queen of Denmark" and "Ophelia, daughter to Polonius," are not mentioned till the end, even though they outrank several of the men listed above them. Does that say something about the power and stature of women in Denmark, or in Shakespearean tragedy, or both? One of them is probably young—she's the "daughter to"—who's Polonius again? Ah, the lord chamberlain. So another way of categorizing people is by their family relationships. How many families do we have here? At least two: Hamlet, his mother, his uncle-stepfather, and the ghost of his father; and Polonius, his son Laertes—another hard name—and his daughter Ophelia. Is Ophelia a child, or will she turn out to be somebody's girlfriend?

There's a priest in the cast, too. Maybe he marries Ophelia off to one of the men—there seem to be a lot of them running around. In fact, this is a *big* cast. But there definitely seem to be starring roles. How can you tell who's important? By how early they're listed in the cast, by their rank and family connection, and by their gender. And by whether or not they have names. For example, who's *not* important? "A Norwegian Captain" and all the "Lords, Ladies, Officers, Soldiers, Sailors, Messengers, Attendants." So Shakespeare's theater had extras, too. But no actresses? All the parts were played by men—oh, and boys? Are you sure? The queen, too?!

No single class would cover all these points. Fewer (or some different ones) will come up, depending on the background and curiosity of the class. The important goal is not to "cover" material but to let the reactions be the students' own, in give-and-take seminar style. Students may well ask some questions that I cannot answer. In my experience, that does not undermine my teacherly authority. We are, after all, engaged in a process of mutual discovery, and students are usually both surprised and pleased at the egalitarian approach. It lets me meet the play without a prepared script and shed the inhibiting conviction that I have to don the expert's mask in order to teach Shakespeare. It makes me, as well as my students, learners.

This technique can work with students of virtually any age or ability level, and with any of Shakespeare's plays. I have concentrated on *Hamlet* because, as a recent survey confirmed, it is the play most frequently taught in American high schools, public, private, and parochial. It is the work most intimately connected with the playwright. On the cover of the Kittredge edition, Shakespeare and his hero are drawn in three-quarter profile, joined at the cheek like Siamese twins. Such lines as "to be or not to be," "the play's the thing," and "the lady doth protest too much" are so well known that it is jarring to see them in context, to realize that someone made them up. Like the *Mona Lisa*, *Hamlet* is alluded to so constantly that the original seems familiar, even to those who have never seen it.

The surprise waiting for students who can get past the monolith of that fame is how fresh the play remains. Hamlet is still a charismatic figure for young readers, as he was for me at their age. Especially in this era of divorce, adolescents identify closely with his dilemma: He must confront his disapproving elders and live up to his own ideals, regardless of the cost. In a way, it is every young person's task, intensified to tragic dimensions. Some students, girls as well as boys, may empathize with one of the other young men in the play—Hamlet's opponent, the fiery Laertes, or Horatio, the stoical confidant of his brilliant, doomed friend. But most will see themselves in Hamlet. For all his supposed thirty years, Hamlet is the quintessential adolescent. I realized early on that I could not *say* any of that. Telling students that Hamlet is an adolescent sounds like condescension, and calling him the most articulate character in literature sounds like an oblique judgment on their verbal skills. The play has to sell itself.

The cast list method should give students a stake in the play, and a new confidence in their ability to read it. They will have listened to their own voices pronouncing Shakespeare's names, mastering the noble titles, getting a sense of the relationships and the issues. Even if they cannot understand everything on a first reading, they can see that the play is written in English, after all. They may have discovered that *Hamlet* is not highfalutin or artsy—that it is "play" in the best sense.

The Short Episode

A useful next step is to turn to the beginning that Shakespeare provided for his own audience: the opening scene. In *Hamlet*, as in all of Shakespeare's best plays, this scene is short and exciting, and it provides a clear introduction not only to the work itself but also to Shakespeare's main dramatic techniques. I often assign Scene i for the first class on *Hamlet*, telling students to read it as carefully as if they were preparing for a quiz. Most will not take that injunction seriously—they're not *really* going to be quizzed, and there is a lot of material to take in. Most will skim the hard parts about Fortinbras, read all the roles in a monotone, and come to class remembering only that the scene features a ghost.

The first scene of Hamlet, like many of Shakespeare's long scenes, is comprised of short episodes, which can be separated, on the classical model, by the entrance of a new speaker. This technique involves casting students in each role and asking them to read aloud as many of these episodes as time allows. Between each one, we pause to answer questions and to talk about what purposes the passage serves. Going slowly over the opening scene this way gives students a chance to see something they may have missed, and helps me decide where they need to go next.

Episode 1, Scene i, Lines 1–13

The first episode is the exchange between Bernardo and Francisco, the two sentinels on duty at the king of Denmark's castle. I ask for volunteers to play these roles—preferably two good readers, but not the best readers in the class. Horatio and Marcellus, who are coming on next, have longer and more demanding parts. On the other hand, if the first readers are so weak that they stumble through the lines, it kills interest and confidence.

I tell the students to read rapidly—one line coming on top of another—to line 13, the entrance of Horatio and Marcellus. I stop someone who completely misreads a line, but I try to let the scene go on without interruption. Most readers warm to the exchange and feel pulled up short when they're reminded to pause at line 13, Horatio's cue to enter. They are usually surprised at how quickly they have become involved in the action. I ask a series of open-ended questions, such as: What does this dialogue accomplish? *Hamlet* begins not with the hero, but with some minor characters: Why? What is the mood of this opening episode? These questions are arranged from least to most specific. Starting with the broadest lets me see what a class can come up with on its own.

The discussion could go in one of several directions, but the main point to establish is the play's opening mood: tense, uncertain, full of foreboding. What in the text suggests such a mood? The time and place contribute: It is midnight (the hour is "now struck twelve") in winter (" 'Tis bitter cold"). The speakers are on guard duty, in itself an edgy situation, and their lines are short and staccato, full of anxious questions. The class may not notice that the first is asked by the wrong man: It is Francisco who is about to go off duty, and therefore he, not Bernardo, should demand, "Who's there?" Francisco's response should emphasize the me: "Nay, answer *me*." It is apt that *Hamlet* begins with a question, and a fearful one at that. But there is more than fear here. What is the key line in this section? Someone is sure to see it: " 'Tis bitter cold,/And I am sick at heart." *Hamlet* begins in despair as well as suspense.

Episode 2, Scene i, Lines 14–39

The second episode adds two new characters, Horatio and Marcellus. I often ask a girl to read one of the roles—Shakespeare, after all, used the opposite means of casting the female roles. If a reader is having trouble, I sometimes ask if a line has been read with the right emphasis. The issue is always whether it is worth breaking the dramatic mood in order to clarify meaning.

What does this new episode accomplish? The most likely answer is that it explains the cause of Francisco and Bernardo's tension. They call it "this thing," then "this dreaded sight," and finally "this apparition." What makes this order effective? Its increasing specificity, which creates suspense.

The other purpose of this episode is to introduce Horatio. How is he revealed to be the most important of the four characters on stage? The others show respect for his rank and defer to his special knowledge: He is the one they hope to convince of the Ghost's appearance. How, then, is Horatio's attitude different from that of the sentries? As they themselves complain, his ears are "fortified against [their] story," which he calls mere "fantasy." His first words reveal him as the skeptic, the rational man who scoffs at the idea of ghosts appearing at midnight. Only "a piece of him" has answered their summons, he tells them: His body is present but his mind holds back.

What is the function of the minor characters? There are several possibilities: to contrast with Horatio; to act as impartial witnesses—all three are "honest soldiers," loyal to their king ("liegemen to the Dane"); to establish the Ghost's authenticity. They have nothing to gain by inventing such a tale—in fact, their knowledge is dangerous. They are simple men, terrified by what they "twice" have seen and yet convinced that they *have* seen it. Before they risk reporting their findings, they want someone of higher authority to "approve [their] eyes." They also want to learn the Ghost's motives for appearing; they want Horatio, the scholar, to "speak to it."

For older or more able students, it is worth pointing out that Shakespeare modulates the rhythm of the speeches in this section with special effectiveness. Several times, spondees—two stressed syllables in a row—are substituted for the regular iambic feet. (A more complete discussion of blank verse is given in Chapter 13.) Francisco's wary hail is made up entirely of spondees: "I think I hear them. Stand, ho! Who is there?" The extra stresses, the monosyllables, and the marked pause in midline (the technical term is "caesura") suggest both that Francisco is shouting and that he is nervous. Spondees create an entirely different tone in Horatio's first question: "What, has this thing appeared again tonight?" Here the extra stresses at the beginning of the line mark the usual inflection for irony in English and underline his skepticism.

Sometimes not the irregularity but the evenness of the rhythm makes a line stand out. One example is Horatio's determinedly calm response to Bernardo's excited demand about whether he is really with them: "A piece of him." The major example of regular meter in the scene is Bernardo's account of the Ghost's first appearance (lines 35–39). How is his diction different from what we have heard till now? Bernardo has launched into the storyteller's mode, and his tone soars with his sense of his importance as star witness:

> *Last night of all,*
> *When yond same star that's westward from the pole*
> *Had made his course t'illumine that part of heaven*
> *Where now it burns...*

With scarcely a pause for breath, Bernardo is giving an elaborate description of a minor detail of setting: in plain words, that a certain star shone at this time on the fateful night. Till this point, the scene has been action-filled and quick-paced, and the language correspondingly direct. Now everything slows down as Bernardo makes the most of his big moment. In the Globe audience, the groundlings would be readying their tomatoes and the nobles their cries of "More matter with less art." How did Shakespeare forestall them? By returning to the action: He cuts short Bernardo's speech with the stage direction "Enter Ghost."

Why does he do that? Because we already know what Bernardo is about to tell us—it is superfluous exposition. "Exposition" is an important enough term to write on the board and define: necessary background information. In drama, unlike fiction, there is no narrator to interrupt the action and explain who the characters are or what events have gone before. All such explanations must be supplied through the dialogue. One mark of a skillful playwright is his or her ability to present exposition smoothly, without calling attention to it or boring the audience. The method works on us as surely as it did on the Elizabethans: the fascination for ghosts has not faded. By this point in the play, students are usually caught up in the action. They should be starting to feel that they understand the language, with some help from the footnotes. They may even be surprised that they once expected *Hamlet* to be highbrow and tedious.

Episode 3, Scene i, Lines 40–69

The third episode extends from the Ghost's entrance to the men's immediate reaction to it. I always cast someone to play the Ghost: it is a silent role in this scene, and so a good means of engaging a student who is shy or bored. If the initial readers are hopeless, or if the class is big, this is a convenient time to recast the other roles. After the reading, I either ask the key question—What is the purpose of this section?—or simply pause until someone starts talking. The discussion is most likely to begin either with the Ghost or with Horatio. If with the former, the salient point is that the Ghost is real: Now still a fourth man, Horatio, has seen him, and we, too, have become eye witnesses. Just as important, we have discovered his identity. He is the spirit of "the King that's dead." We learn that he was a consummate soldier. He is clad in "armour," his "stalk" is "martial," his "frown" is "angry," a description that evokes his past battles with Norway and Poland. Horatio recalls times that he "smote" these enemies. This exposition is so dramatic that the old king springs to life.

How does Horatio react to the Ghost? Confronted with the actuality, rather than the mere rumor, he admits, "It harrows me with fear and wonder." The key word, "harrows," literally means "plows up" with a heavy, spiked implement. As so often in Shakespeare, the verb is both forceful and vivid, a metaphor in a single word. Yet Horatio maintains enough of his composure to address the spirit with formal courtesy. When it refuses to respond, he again loses control and cries, "Stay! Speak, speak! I charge thee speak!" How does Shakespeare convey the desperation in that cry? It is all monosyllables, all spondees, all exclamations, and the form of address lapses into the familiar "thee." Horatio is a rational man but no ice-blooded stoic.

Where else do we see an indication of Horatio's feelings? After the Ghost has gone off, Bernardo cannot resist vindicating himself: "How now, Horatio? You tremble and look pale./ Is not this something more than fantasy?" In Shakespeare, everything is contained in the dialogue: the identity of the characters, the settings, and, as in this case, the stage directions. The play can come alive in a reading because it is all there to *be* read. How do we feel about Horatio now? Most readers like him and trust him. He has refused to be prey to superstition, to believe that the Ghost exists "Without," he says, "the sensible and true avouch/Of mine own eyes." But once he has this proof, he immediately starts to speculate on the meaning of the spirit's appearance. He alone sees the larger implication: "This bodes some strange eruption to our state." Horatio is a man to respect, but, as the title reveals, this is not *his* tragedy. This first scene makes us curious about the role that Horatio will play.

Episode 4, Scene i, Lines 70–125

This episode is the one most likely to cause trouble: a long passage of exposition on the state of the kingdom, set up by Marcellus's series of questions about the "sweaty haste" with which Denmark is preparing for war. It is difficult to follow because the language is formal and complex, because a modern audience is likely to know little about the Hamlet legend or the rules of medieval combat (e.g., what does it mean that a prebattle agreement was "well ratified by law and heraldry"?), and because there turn out to be two generations of Hamlets and Fortinbrases to keep straight. It is not a quick read.

Nevertheless, students usually decipher the main point: The purpose of all this military preparation is to defend Denmark against young Fortinbras's threatened invasion. The Norwegian prince is determined to win back lands that his father, old Fortinbras, lost in single combat against old Hamlet. The fact that the combat was both legitimate and fairly conducted does not deter Fortinbras. He wants both to regain the lands and to avenge his father, who was slain in the duel. Old Fortinbras's conqueror, old Hamlet, has since become the Ghost we have just seen stalking the battlements. He is first referred to simply as "Hamlet" (line 84), so some students will confuse him with the hero, who has not yet been mentioned.

How does Shakespeare try to make this exposition both clear and interesting? One answer—suggested above—is that he saves it until this point in the first scene, when he has already engaged our attention through the action. He also makes the account as clear as possible by putting it in the mouth of the most intelligent witness, Horatio. He explains the essentials in what is really a little essay: background information, present situation, conclusion. Lest we miss a point, he repeats key ideas: e.g., in the final six lines of his exposition, Horatio reiterates that the Danes are arming against young Fortinbras's invasion, and he says in three synonymous phrases that this is the "main motive" of the very "watch" they are sharing. Horatio further engages our attention by the sensationalism of his story and the vigor of his language. He is reporting the "whisper" he has heard—a word that suggests the suspicion and fear rampant in Denmark—an account of boldness, treachery, and overweening pride. His verbs create an animated picture of both generations of Fortinbrases, the elder "prick'd on by a most emulate pride" to "dare" his Danish rival to single combat, the son moved by similar motives to "shark up" mercenaries to win back the lands his father lost. This last metaphor of voracity is carried through three lines (98–100).

The assumption made by all three men is that the impending military crisis has caused the Ghost "that was and is the question of these wars" to walk the earth. We who have read *Hamlet* before know that this is a red herring, that the view of young Fortinbras will change completely as the play goes on. This is not to be a history play, a reenactment of the old kings' struggle in the present generation. The play's true focus is implied in Horatio's long analogy between the atmosphere in Denmark and the supernatural events in ancient Rome just before Julius Caesar fell. My students often dismiss this passage as Horatio the scholar's inability to resist a historical allusion. In fact, it is an example of the dramatic irony that Shakespeare often achieves through classical references that imply more than the speaker intends. Here, the Elizabethan audience would know that Caesar, like old Hamlet, was murdered, and by someone he trusted. Calling students' attention to this point would spoil the plot—they, like Horatio, know nothing yet of the Danish regicide. It is enough to note Horatio's tone: How does he feel about the Ghost's appearance? In a word, queasy. He calls it an evil omen, the "precurse of fear'd events." His premise—that the manifestation is connected with Fortinbras—may be wrong, but his conclusion will prove all too accurate.

Episode 5, Scene i, Lines 126–75

Horatio suddenly interrupts his speculations with an explosion of exclamations: The Ghost has reappeared. Again, action replaces exposition. What is the purpose of this final episode? It adds no new information—with one important exception. Someone usually notices that it introduces the character of "young Hamlet" (line 170). Horatio suggests reporting their encounter to him. The natural question is, why save the first reference to the hero for the end of this scene? The best answers are that it increases the suspense and raises his stature. Horatio, who has shown himself a man of wisdom and courage, believes that the spirit which has remained mute in spite of all their efforts will speak to the prince. They must report to Hamlet, he urges, "as needful in our loves, fitting our duty."

What is our impression of Horatio in this second encounter with the Ghost? His behavior reinforces our earlier positive opinion. He shows a great deal of knowledge about the reasons that ghosts "walk in death," and he addresses this one with resolution and respect. But he is human enough to lose his composure a second time when the spirit flees at the cock's crow. He urges Marcellus to strike at it with his halberd. In a nice bit of psychological realism, it is Marcellus, the homely soldier, who sets the standard of conduct this time. He upbraids them all for treating the Ghost with "malicious mockery."

This direct experience of the supernatural does not destroy Horatio's healthy skepticism: He accepts only "in part" the superstitions about witches and fairies that Marcellus pours forth. Finally, Horatio shows his poetic side. He can appreciate the beauty of dawning day and describe it in homely metaphor as "clad" in "russet mantle." What practical purpose does this description serve? There was neither lighting nor scenery in Shakespeare's theater: Midnight and dawn alike were staged in the midafternoon light. The setting occurred in the words of the actors and the imaginations of the spectators.

Ending the Beginning

This introduction to the play should not take longer than two class periods. If it can be done in one, so much the better. The goal is not to cover all the points made above, nor to cover them in that neat order: Even the attempt would mean sacrificing spontaneity to thoroughness. In a classroom dialogue, digressions are not only inevitable but also valuable, and the course of a discussion depends on what students are seeing and asking. I have found that a scene never teaches the same way, even in back-to-back classes. But my goals in these introductory exercises remain the same: to make students more comfortable with the language, more curious about the plot, and more insightful towards the characters. Now they need to be pushed out of the nest and shown that they can fly through *Hamlet* on their own—how fast depends on the age and the ability of the class.

A sure method of encouraging active reading is the old-fashioned quiz. Older students—juniors through adults—can handle a quiz on all of Act I. Younger or less able students need a slower pace—either a quiz on only the first three scenes, including the one that we have gone over, or another day of the dramatic reading/discussion of episodes technique before being quizzed. I remind students that they did not, after all, have a quiz on Scene i, but add that tomorrow they *will* have one. The format is simple: six short questions of fact and interpretation, including at least one quotation to identify. Before panic sets in, I divert students' nervous energy into inventing some possible questions about the scene we have just read: What is the identity of the Ghost? Why is Fortinbras preparing to attack Denmark? Who says, and to whom, "A piece of him"? Describe Horatio in three adjectives. I tell them to read the assignment at least twice, the second time out loud, if possible. Finally, I assure them the quiz will not "count" much in terms of grades, but that it will be an important measure of how carefully they read.

Chapter 3

The Quiz Revisited: *Hamlet*

As the class settles down, I say, "Take out a sheet of paper and a pen. The quiz has six questions, five main ones and a bonus. I'll ask each one out loud, repeat it once if necessary, and give you time to write your answer. These are short-answer questions—some can be covered in a word or a phrase, and no response should be more than two sentences long. You'll get partial credit for any part of an answer that's right. Ready? Question one..." Here's a sample quiz:

1. Name three issues that Claudius deals with in his opening audience.
2. What order does Polonius give to Ophelia?
3. Name three wrongs that the Ghost accuses Claudius of.
4. Who says this, and to whom or in what situation? "Frailty, thy name is woman."
5. "He waxes desperate with imagination." Name some point in Act I where Horatio's description of Hamlet's behavior applies.

Bonus question: Name two potential conflicts that Act I introduces. Put them in this form: _____ vs. _____.

This quiz is designed for an older class—juniors and up—with at least average verbal ability. The answers to the questions, as well as a discussion of their implications, appear in the final section of this chapter. First, I explain how the quiz works.

The Form of the Questions

Each quiz takes a standard but not rigid form: six questions on key aspects of character, plot, theme, and language. At least one of the questions is a quotation, for which the student has to identify both speaker and listener (or situation). Questions of this type have only one right answer. Others have a range of acceptable answers—e.g., "Describe Polonius in three adjectives." Some may be wide open: "A good subtitle for Act II would be ..." I try to make the set of questions cover as many aspects of the act as possible. So, a quiz that contained a quotation by Polonius would not also ask for a description of him in three adjectives. If I have two class sections, I might give one class the first question and the other the second, so that each quiz would touch on Polonius as parent or royal advisor or both. These are not essay questions: The best require an answer of not more than a sentence. Nor should they be tricky. They should be challenging but straightforward enough to reward even the plodding student who could not, for example, write a cogent essay on Polonius but who can describe the old man as "nosy," "talkative," and "bossy."

Writing the Questions

In making up a question, I may start with just a general observation—for example, that Claudius and Gertrude have a troubled relationship with Hamlet. Then I ask myself if I can turn that point into a question, and, if so, how I can focus it. One possibility is to ask for a brief description of Hamlet's attitude toward the king. But that is likely to evoke too long and vague an answer. Another is to ask students to identify Hamlet's first sarcastic comment on his uncle-stepfather: "A little more than kin, and less than kind!" That is more specific, but if several of the other questions are also about Hamlet, it would put too much emphasis on his character. I finally decide to ask, "What are two ploys that Claudius uses to try to win Hamlet over?" That question is the hardest, but it focuses on Claudius, and so both provides variety and implies something about the king's shrewdness.

I vary the quiz process according to the needs of the class. I may start slowly, going over the entire first act in class, inventing practice questions along the way. I usually give one quiz per act, but, if the reading is difficult or the class slow, I give a quiz only on the second half of an act. For similar reasons, I will ask a hard question in an easier form—by quoting more of a passage students are to identify or by asking for only one proof of a point. Before the quiz, I sometimes let students ask questions on vocabulary and syntax—the literal meaning of words and phrases. This format can be unwieldy: Students might anticipate part of the quiz, so I have to prepare alternate versions of questions—e.g., a factual question and a quotation that cover the same topic. Other students might ask questions simply in the hope of delaying the test. The discussion is often lively but less thoughtful than one that follows a quiz, and certainly less disinterested. But it can be a valuable learning tool, especially for conscientious readers and good listeners.

I keep the scoring simple—one point per question, with fractional credit for any part of an answer that is right. That policy rewards all understanding of the play and persuades students that the quiz is fair. I usually give a bonus question in addition to the basic five, so that the possible total score is 6 (120%). Finally, I count the average of the five quiz grades as equivalent to only one test. My goal is that by the third quiz, nearly everyone will be making at least a 3. In other words, I want this to be a success story for most students.

The Teacher as Student

Although students may not realize it, when I devise and they study for a quiz, both of us are participating in the same process: working to understand the play's language, isolate the key issues, interpret the characters' actions, and see the structural patterns. The purpose of the quiz is not to trap students with questions about petty details, as some will inevitably suspect. Nor is it to cover every aspect of an act: No group of six questions could be so thorough. The purpose is to make students read with attention and imagination. For every question that actually appears on the quiz, the student should have anticipated it in some form, and thought of three more besides. The best questions prod students not only into sharpening their understanding but even into realizing something that they did not know they knew. In my turn, I try to see the play again as I saw it once: with the eyes of a new reader. I ask myself what in a given act students must understand, and which speeches are most likely to puzzle or mislead. Is there a line I do not understand? Is it worth researching or asking a colleague about, or would it be a useful point for class discussion?

In making up a quiz, it saves time to take notes as I read—on possible questions or apt quotations or simply on what a scene covers. I look over these notes afterwards and try to think of the questions in categories. A major one is characterization. Because the Globe, like other London theaters of its day, had a repertory company, Shakespeare, its main playwright-in-residence, created roles tailored to his fellow members: the tragic hero, the witty fool, the old father, the short, clever girl. Yet as Shakespeare wrote them, these are not stereotypes. The same boy apprentice who played Ophelia, for example, might possibly have played Juliet, Portia, and Viola. Each of these short, clever girls has her own distinctive voice. But how can I help students "hear" it on the page, without the aid of gesture, tone, and facial expression? By asking some key questions: Does each speech seem characteristic of the speaker? If not, what is causing the change in diction or tone? Would it be possible to read the speech in more than one way? Which lines are essential to the action? Which add undercurrents of meaning? Are any words or ideas repeated, and if so, why? Are any of the lines famous? Do such lines take on a different meaning in the context of the play?

Once I have begun to decipher, I also begin to compare, and so to perceive patterns in the play's structure. Shakespeare often uses juxtaposition to suggest a contrast: between conflicting attitudes in the same character—Macbeth's scruples and his ambition, Ophelia's love for Hamlet and her sense of duty to her father; between characters, such as Prince Hal and Hotspur, Viola and Olivia, Hamlet and Claudius; between worlds, such as Rome and Egypt, the court and the greenwood, earth and purgatory. A tragic episode often follows a comic one; a big public scene, a tête-à-tête. There is often a contrast between what a character says to others and what he admits in soliloquy, between what he professes and how he acts, between his level of diction in one situation and in another. For example, Hamlet makes skilled and solemn use of courtly diction in praising Fortinbras, but parodies it in mocking Osric. Shakespeare uses all these patterns of contrast to imply meaning, so I try to devise questions that get students to see them.

Finally, the playwright implies meaning through the order in which he presents scenes and introduces characters. Here, some crucial questions are the following: At what point in the action does a character appear? How do we gauge importance: by the amount of time that she remains on stage? By the number of lines that she speaks? By the characters she addresses? By whether she dies or marries on stage or off? How does the point at which a scene occurs affect our reaction to it? (For example, Claudius's glittering first audience is made darkly ironic by the Ghost's accusation of murder and usurpation, which follows shortly after.) What is a typical resolution for a tragedy? A comedy? At what point does the action turn irretrievably in a tragic or comic direction? Again, I want the quiz questions to touch on as many of these techniques as possible, so that students are learning not only what a play means but also—to borrow a phrase from the critic and poet John Ciardi—*how* it means.

After the Quiz

I use the quiz questions as the basis for the rest of that day's discussion, listening to gauge the general reaction to the questions and to see how fully the class has understood the reading. The following day, when I return the quizzes, I call on students to read answers that are especially clear or imaginative. As often as possible, I choose people who do not think of themselves as Shakespeare buffs—who may have only one excellent answer on a whole quiz. Some of the subtlest insights in my own classes have come from students who, in the beginning, were deaf to nuances of tone and character. The further that they got in the play, the more they were able to hear, and to take pride in that ability. Succeeding on a Shakespeare quiz was for them a small but heady triumph—the first step in responding more appreciatively to other hard books as well.

But if several students seem puzzled or frustrated, I may vary the quiz format: slow the reading pace; give an optional make-up quiz, comprised mostly of quotations to identify; devise a face-off among students who have answered the six questions correctly; ask the student with the highest score to make up the next quiz for everyone, including me; put every student in the position of quiz-maker, by asking them to invent a question or to cite a quotation that they expected to see on that day's quiz. I may also have individual or group conferences with students who are having trouble; watch and discuss scenes from a videotaped performance of the act; or substitute an in-class essay or a mime exercise (see Chapter 4) for one of the quizzes.

Occasionally, someone who is working hard simply has a deaf ear for dialogue. The indication is often that this student wildly misidentifies the quotations even though he gets the other questions right. I advise such students to read out loud and, if possible, to tape and play back their own voices. Puzzling out the rhythm of a line usually conveys more of its meaning than listening passively to an actor delivering it. For some, though, a recording of the play can be a real ear-opener.

If a student misses a quiz, I may ask her to devise one of her own. Then I evaluate the questions for variety and precision: Do they really demand short answers rather than little essays? Do they cover the main aspects of the plot, the characterization, and the language? I usually grade the student quiz holistically, on the plus-check-minus system.

Two class periods are usually sufficient to cover an act. With a slower pace, discussion drags and students lose track of the plot. On the other hand, a single period is usually too short to cover the main issues. There is no hard rule: I try to make the pace fast enough to keep interest high, but not so fast that people get confused and discouraged. A major advantage of the quiz technique is that it creates mutual empathy. It makes both teacher and student read the play through the other one's eyes. It also lets me be better prepared—more familiar with the text, more flexible. Having read closely the passages that I am to teach the next day, I am readier to anticipate misunderstandings and to see issues from different angles, readier to discuss than to hold forth. Grading the quiz shows me issues and lines that need to be clarified. Going over the answers in class gives students a chance to play the authority. I have found this process so valuable that I make up a new set of quizzes, or refine an old one, every time I teach the first play of the semester.

The Answers to the Questions on Act I

Question 1. Name three issues that Claudius deals with in his opening audience.

The initial reaction to this questions is often a startled "Huh?" Students read Claudius's first scene without knowing that he is Hamlet's great enemy. It is only in returning to Claudius's words, after hearing the Ghost's revelations, that students can judge the king's words accurately. Those who have not taken the trouble to reread probably will not remember much of this key episode. What they will recall is likely to be an oversimplification: that Claudius talks in a "phony" way. Beginning with what he says rather than how he says it forces students to get their facts straight before they try to evaluate them.

Under the pressure of a quiz, many students realize that they do in fact remember some of the ideas that Claudius brought up as he went on and on. There was that guy who wanted to go back to France—what was his name? Yeah—Laertes going back to France. Oh, and the invasion—that other guy is threatening to invade Denmark and Claudius doesn't like it. And Hamlet is giving him a hard time about old Hamlet, so Claudius puts Hamlet down—"unmanly grief" he calls it. And of course the real reason Hamlet's ticked is that his mother has married this jerk—hey, that's another issue—the new marriage. One, two, three—do I get extra credit for four?

After the quiz, there will inevitably be controversy about which answers are correct: *Did* Claudius deal with a particular issue? I turn such questions back to the class: Where in the play do we go to find out? We turn to the court scene (ii), and either I or a talented student reads Claudius's long opening speech, pausing each time the king introduces a new topic.

The class can signal the pauses, calling "Stop!" when Claudius switches issues. I also ask students to note the order of the topics Claudius takes up and the style in which he discusses them. This is the man, I remind them, that we later discover has murdered his brother to become king. What is Shakespeare implying about Claudius's feelings and abilities?

The first issue that Claudius confronts is the recent death of his brother and predecessor. This is the new king's first big public audience. Everyone who is anyone in Denmark is there—the courtiers, the lord chamberlain and his family, the prince royal. What tone does Claudius take? He is solemn, formal, presumably grieving within but calm and dignified without. How does the *way* that he talks reflect those qualities? Any group of modern students is likely to be put off by Claudius's elevated diction and complex syntax. Their temptation is to dismiss his rhetoric because it is difficult to understand. Before the discussion dissolves into wisecracks about the obscurity of Claudius's speech, I try to get students to figure out why the tone sounds so formal. The best answers are the use of the royal *we*, the balance of the clauses, the regularity of the meter, and the elaborate figures of speech. Claudius does not stop at simple metaphors. He uses a synecdoche that reduces the "whole kingdom" to one eyebrow frowning in grief, and a series of oxymorons that express such paradoxes as "wisest sorrow" and "defeated joy." Is this diction "phony"? Out of place for the occasion? How would Claudius's audience hear it? Claudius is speaking eloquent solemnities perfectly fitting for a Renaissance monarch on a high state occasion. At the same time, the students' instincts are right. As hindsight tells us, Shakespeare is using this highly polished rhetoric to imply that Claudius is as insincere as he is poised.

Does the king give himself away at any point? The line "we with wisest sorrow think on him/Together with remembrance of ourselves" reads like an unwitting double entendre. Claudius's golden tongue is forked. But it is important that at this point in the tragedy no one except the king himself knows that. An actor might play Claudius as a soap opera villain, but most make him seem a charismatic and regal figure. Not only is a sincere-sounding Claudius more subtle, but also such an interpretation raises his stature, and so indirectly raises Hamlet's. If Claudius is just "a king of shreds and patches," his rival cannot seriously fear him, and his caution in seeking revenge becomes ludicrous. Thus, hypocrite though he is, Claudius should express his grief with dignity and conviction.

The second issue that the new king takes up is stickier: his marriage to his former sister-in-law. Why is that union controversial? It was made less than a month after the death of the new king's brother and, more important, in Elizabethan canon law it was considered incestuous. Hamlet stresses both these points with bitter irony in his first exchange with Horatio. So why doesn't Claudius ignore this awkward issue altogether? Because he is too shrewd a politician. He paints the widow's haste in taking up with her brother-in-law in patriotic colors: Gertrude has brought Claudius the "dowry" of her dead husband's kingdom and thus prevented any grappling for the throne. She is, he claims with a hyperbolic flourish, "the imperial jointress to this warlike state." He does not, of course, mention the rightful heir, who was away at school in Wittenberg during all these upheavals and is now glowering darkly at this very assemblage. How else does Claudius use his skill at rhetoric to win over his keenly attentive court? He expresses the supposed ambivalence of the new royal couple in oxymorons: They have acted "with mirth in funeral, and with dirge in marriage." Again, the paradoxes are both appropriate to the situation and indicative of the new king's hypocrisy. Finally, Claudius implicates his courtiers in the match, complimenting them for "freely" approving of "this affair." He concludes with royal magnanimity: "For all, our thanks." In a matter of sixteen lines, Claudius has glossed over two potential scandals and flattered both his bride and his courtiers.

But the king is too clever to linger over loaded issues. What is his next ploy? In a word, diversion. He deftly turns from internal affairs of state to external: young Fortinbras's threatened invasion. How does Claudius use this real but convenient problem to his own best advantage? He ascribes to his country's enemy the worst view of the new reign: The Norwegian prince holds "a weak supposal of our worth" and believes Denmark to be "disjoint and out of frame" after old Hamlet's death. We have just been shown that Fortinbras's judgment is exactly right: Something is rotten in this state. But the courtiers have not heard that the old king's ghost is stalking the land. To them, Claudius's contempt for the young foreigner's presumptuousness must seem eminently real. Claudius then hurries on to tell the court—and us—that the present ruler of Norway, Fortinbras's uncle, is ignorant of his nephew's aggression. He dispatches ambassadors to inform Norway of the situation and to demand that the Norwegian ruler "suppress" the "gait" of his ambitious nephew. What impression would this action make on the Danish courtiers? Claudius has just dealt swiftly and skillfully with the chief foreign issue of his new reign. He seems every inch a king.

What issue does he take up next? The request of Laertes to return to the pleasures of life in France. How does that compare with the problems that Claudius has just dealt with? It is a simple domestic matter. Laertes is an appealing young noble, his services are apparently not needed at court, and his fond father has no objections to his going. How does Claudius treat this rubber-stamp request? He turns on the young man the full power of his charm: "What wouldst thou beg, Laertes,/That shall not be my offer, not thy asking?" How does Claudius's diction change to suit this situation? He uses "thou," the old familiar form of "you," the singular "my," instead of the royal "our," and the balance of "offer" and "asking"—to create an intimate tone. What image is he trying to project? This is the warm, generous monarch, who rewards loyal service with royal favor.

How does Laertes respond? Exactly as Claudius would wish. He addresses the king as "My dread lord," affirms his "duty" to Claudius, and asks the king's "gracious leave and pardon" to depart. After a pretense of asking Polonius's permission, Claudius grants the request with hearty magnanimity: "Take thy fair hour, Laertes." Why has Claudius taken up this issue at this point? One reason, as implied above, is that the actor in him senses that it is time to show his public a softer side: the king-as-affectionate-father after the king-as-bold-leader. Just as important, Claudius is mindful of the thorny issue that remains to be faced: how to appease his contrary new stepson. Clearly, he hopes that the courtesy shown by Laertes will rub off on Hamlet. Should that fail, Claudius has at least made his court witness to the kingly generosity he can show to a young man capable of appreciating it.

The confrontation between Claudius and Hamlet is complex enough that it could be the subject of an alternate first quiz question: "Name two means by which Claudius attempts to win Hamlet over during his opening audience." Again, to follow the king's ploys, it helps to read out loud part of the exchange between the prince and his parents (lines 64–128), stopping at each new technique that Claudius tries. The first is affectionate cajoling. He calls Hamlet "my son" and asks, "How is it that the clouds still hang on you?" Why doesn't he ignore the fact that Hamlet is still openly mourning for his father? Again, because Claudius is too wily to deny the obvious. Instead, as with the question of his hasty incestuous marriage, he confronts the situation and tries to outface it. Does that tactic work on the prince? No; it backfires completely.

Hamlet responds with an oration on "all forms, moods, shapes of grief" that stresses the distinction between feigned and deeply felt sorrow. This is clearly a dig at the king and queen. Now it is Claudius's move. What does he do? He meets criticism with criticism. In fact, he goes Hamlet one better: He berates the young man openly. Such grief as Hamlet displays, Claudius argues, is "unmanly," a wrong against "heaven," "the dead," "nature," and "reason." Does Shakespeare signal Claudius's hypocrisy at any point in this passionate argument? Since death is "common," Claudius echoes Gertrude, "Why should we .../Take it to heart?" Again, there is an unwitting double entendre: The murderer is implying his own heartlessness.

How does Hamlet respond to this tirade? Not at all—Claudius gives him no chance. Again, the king switches from the stick to the carrot: He names Hamlet "the most immediate to our throne." Though Denmark is an elective monarchy, the present king's voice is powerful support for the succession. Isn't this a generous offer? In a word, no. Hamlet should be reigning *now*, not after his uncle. This is the be-a-good-boy-and-you'll-get-back-what-I-stole-from-you-*later* ploy. Does Claudius stop there? No; he goes back to painting his feelings toward Hamlet in fatherly colors, addressing the prince as "son" twice and referring to himself as "father" twice in the last ten lines of his speech, and begging Hamlet to remain at court rather than return to Wittenberg.

What is Hamlet's reaction to this eloquent bribe? He says nothing. How might this moment be directed? In some way that showed Hamlet's sullenness and Claudius's embarrassment—the prince's silence should be long and awkward. Neither of the men breaks it: Gertrude does. In some consternation, she adds her pleading to her husband's, to which Hamlet replies: "I shall in all my best obey you, madam." How are we to hear that answer? It is addressed only to Gertrude, it ignores all mention of the succession, and its tone is grudging. The words could hardly be more slighting to Claudius. Does the king object? Not on his kingship. Instead, he seizes on the chance to end a humiliating public scene. He pronounces Hamlet's half-hearted statement "a loving and a fair reply." Then he says with feigned jollity that he will celebrate the prince's "gentle and unforced accord" with rousing toasts marked by firings of the "great cannon." Thus, Claudius disguises his vexation with smooth speech and promised spectacle, and makes a quick exit before the heir apparent can do further damage to his public image.

No one class discussion would cover all these points. But students should emerge with a clearer sense of Claudius's predicament, and of his powers. Reviewing this scene after reading the Ghost's account of the murder to young Hamlet three scenes later (I. v. 35–80) makes clear the pressure that the new king must have been under. Yet, in spite of his private guilt and fear of public exposure, Claudius appears self-possessed, quick, and wily. He deals with the problems facing his new reign in a deliberate and clever order, with the clear aim of winning over his new subjects. In this first appearance, Claudius shows himself to be an expert actor, a shrewd politician, and a formidable enemy to Hamlet.

Question 2. What order does Polonius give to Ophelia?

This is a question of specific fact: Polonius commands his daughter "in plain terms" to avoid all future "words or talk" (I. iii. 131–35) with Hamlet. On the level of information, the question requires getting characters' names straight—some students will still be confusing Polonius and Claudius or Ophelia and Gertrude. It also means understanding an important turn in the plot: Polonius's order is the initial cause of Hamlet's alienation from Ophelia. On the level of interpretation, the reason for asking this question is to suggest other, more complicated questions: Why does Polonius's order have such a devastating effect on the love affair? Answer: Not so much because of the father's command as because of the daughter's strict obedience to it. What, then, is Ophelia like? An alternate question, which focuses on Ophelia's character, rather than on her father's, would be: "Describe Ophelia in three adjectives." The answers might include gentle, obedient, docile, unassertive, even fearful or embarrassed. Although this is more a question of nuance than of fact, not every response is right. Once, a student tried to argue that "blonde" was acceptable because Ophelia seemed like a "blonde type." Someone else shot back, "You mean, a bombshell?" and the argument dissolved in laughter. It is a student myth that any interpretation is right if someone sincerely believes it. When in doubt, I go back to the text. If a reader can make a convincing case that an idea is implied in the lines, she or he deserves credit—or perhaps partial credit. The important point to make here is that Ophelia receives Polonius's order just as he would have her do: The authoritarian father has raised a subservient daughter.

Is Ophelia simply a product of her times—a typical young woman of Shakespeare's day? That oversimplification can be corrected by recalling some of Shakespeare's other heroines, such as Viola, Rosalind, and Portia—witty, resourceful, and self-reliant, every one. Probably the one most familiar to modern students is Juliet. Had Shakespeare chosen to make Ophelia more like Juliet, she would have defied her father to aid her lover, and *Hamlet* would be a different play. But Ophelia never falters in her filial duty. What is the result? As his first soliloquy shows, Hamlet is already feeling misogynous because of his mother's fickleness. When his beloved turns him away, he must feel that he is being betrayed on all sides, and that he has to face his terrible situation alone. There is no indication that he ever confides in Ophelia, on stage or off. By the end of the first act, the love story in *Hamlet* has been eclipsed by the revenge tragedy.

Why does Polonius separate the lovers? Is he acting out of malice? Not at all. He thinks that he has Ophelia's best interests at heart. What goes wrong? Polonius's view of both his daughter and her interests. He sees Ophelia as a "green girl," a "woodcock" in "perilous" danger of being caught in the "springes" of Hamlet's false "vows"—in other words, an innocent dupe who will be seduced and abandoned. Is this concern entirely benevolent? His own reputation is also at stake, Polonius reminds Ophelia, and he would have her act "as it behooves my daughter and your honour." What does this line suggest about Polonius's view of a daughter's chastity? That it is the father's property, and that she must guard it as much as for his sake as for her own. Does Ophelia simply accept this view? She keeps trying in her mild way to protest. For example, she says that Hamlet has courted her "in honourable fashion." Polonius's reaction? He seizes on the word "fashion," and twists it to mean "whim."

Why can't Polonius believe that Hamlet's love for Ophelia is honorable? One reason is pragmatic: Hamlet is of a higher social station and so could not hope to improve his status through such a marriage. Why could this not be love for love's sake? Because, Polonius argues, everyone knows that young men are promiscuous. His reasoning goes: Young man plus young woman equals seduction. He assures Ophelia:

> *I do know,*
> *When the blood burns, how prodigal the soul*
> *Lends the tongue vows.*

How does he know? Because, these lines imply, the young Polonius was such a seducer. Just as important, this is the view of young men that conventional wisdom dictates. In other words, Polonius judges other people on the basis of personal experience and of stereotype. Here, the two coincide. How does he treat Ophelia when she tries to suggest a more idealistic view of young love? "Pooh!" he exclaims. "You speak like a green girl." His tone is peremptory and scornful.

Why does Ophelia accept this advice? It sounds familiar—have we heard it earlier in the play? Yes—in Ophelia's tête-à-tête with Laertes, which directly precedes this scene with Polonius. What do the father's and son's attitudes have in common? Both see material gain as the primary motive for marriage. On the open market, Laertes implies, Ophelia is an "unvalued person," and Polonius says outright that she must not accept Hamlet's "tenders" ("offers" as well as money, "legal tender") "for true pay." Exactly as his father does, Laertes tries to persuade Ophelia that Hamlet's love can only be "the trifling of his favour," a "toy in the blood"—whimsical and transient. Are there other similarities between the men's attitudes? Even in diction, Laertes is his father's son. He anticipates two of Polonius's metaphors—fire, to describe the passion of the youthful lover, and war, to picture the maiden as the besieged castle. She must stay "Out of the shot and danger of desire" if she is to guard her "chaste treasure." Polonius later argues that, should Ophelia negotiate a surrender, it should be "a higher rate" than a mere "command to parley."

How is the advice of Laertes different from that of his father? It is couched in softer language. He speaks to his sister with gentleness and gallantry. His most frequent metaphor is the spring flower, in danger of being blighted before it can bloom. How else does he soften the advice? He is more tentative, both in describing the problem and in telling her how to cope with it. He concedes of Hamlet's feelings, "Perhaps he loves you now," though he stresses that the prince's "greatness" does not leave him free to marry whom he would. Having warned Ophelia to "be wary," Laertes leaves the choice of how to act to her: He gives no commands.

How does Ophelia respond to her brother? She is much more self-possessed, much less credulous. She mocks his high moral tone and even his favorite floral metaphor: If he will show her "the steep and thorny way to heaven," he must not himself amble along "the primrose path of dalliance." Why is she able to see through Laertes? Perhaps because of his affectionate manner, perhaps because they are so close in age. By Polonius's own implication, he was as lusty a youth as his son, yet Ophelia never confronts him. In her answer to him, there is no protest, no teasing—only acquiescence. It is not in her nature to judge her father.

Just before this scene with Ophelia, we have heard Polonius give his famous advice to his son. He concludes with this precept: "This above all—to thine own self be true, / And it must follow, as the night the day, / Thou canst not then be false to any man." How does this sentiment apply to Polonius's treatment of Ophelia? There is a flagrant contradiction here. In ordering Ophelia to reject Hamlet, Polonius forces her to betray her own convictions of her lover's "truth." Is Polonius a hypocrite? Not at all. Simply, he is a man of business, whether the subject is borrowing money or conducting courtship. So what is Polonius's often-quoted speech to his son about? It is worth pausing to read it aloud. Polonius's advice is about making one's way in the world—establishing and maintaining the right image, getting ahead. It is about shrewdness and economy, even in friendship. Its central virtue is self-interest, its emotional motor the conviction that proverbial wisdom is all-sufficient. Living by certain conventional premises, Polonius asserts, people can always be confident that they are right and that their actions are honorable.

What is missing from this view? In a word, imagination. Polonius is incapable of realizing that things can be seen from more than one angle. Where does the play present a contrast to his simplistic outlook? In Hamlet's restless seeking. As Hamlet says in his first soliloquy, bitter experience has caused him to see beyond and to dismiss "all the uses of this world." After Hamlet has heard the Ghost's revelations, his first vow is to eschew "all saws of books"—the very platitudes that Polonius is forever quoting. There can be more than one truth, more than one duty, even more than one self, to which to be true. Ophelia can fulfill her father's command only by betraying her lover. Polonius does not even see that there is a conflict.

Question 3. Name three wrongs that the Ghost accuses Claudius of.

This is another question of fact rather than interpretation. Where do we turn to find the answer? To the Ghost's long account to his awe-stricken son (I. v.). There are more than the three answers asked for: murder, usurpation, incest, adultery, falsehood (Claudius has presented a "forged" account of King Hamlet's death "to the whole ear of Denmark"), and denying the victim a chance for confession and absolution.

Most of these wrongs are universal. Are there any that might puzzle a modern audience? Both the business about absolution and the reference to incest probably need explanation. The first might suggest to students that the victim is guiltier than in fact he is; the second that the murderer is more innocent than he seemed to Shakespeare's audience. The Ghost's literally hair-raising account of purgatory often leads students to think that the "imperfections" on his "head" when Claudius's poison went to work were considerable. Thus, they conclude, young Hamlet is wrong to idealize a man who is actually as villainous as Claudius. I stress that, according to the religious doctrine of the time, even a man who had led an essentially virtuous life was subject to the purifying torments of purgatory if he died without confessing. This doctrine explains Hamlet's later hesitation to kill Claudius when he finds him praying, and thus, presumably, in a condition of grace: True revenge must exact equal pains. As for incest, most editions of the play provide a footnote supporting the Ghost's accusation: The Elizabethans considered marriage to one's brother's wife an incestuous bond. Gertrude is not literally Claudius's sister, but in the eyes of the Church her sin in marrying him is as great as if she were.

Why ask this question? The main reason is to make clear the complex nature of Claudius's guilt: It is based on more than fratricide. Furthermore, the new king's sins are real: We have "the Ghost's word" for them, not just the prince's suspicions. Another reason is to suggest that the Ghost's judgment of the new king parallels his son's: Hamlet's scorn has an otherworldly echo. The Ghost calls Claudius a "serpent," an "adulterate beast," and "a wretch whose natural gifts were poor/To those of mine." Gertrude's love for her former brother-in-law is "a falling-off" that reduces the "royal bed of Denmark" to "a couch for luxury and damned incest." Their lovemaking is analogous to "prey[ing] on garbage." What is striking about this language? The speaker is a supernatural being, yet the vehemence of his tone and the vividness of his metaphors are very much of this world. Do they have a parallel in the play? Again, the analogy is with young Hamlet's revulsion for Gertrude's new marriage. Like Laertes, Hamlet is his father's son.

But, as the next lines suggest, he is no carbon copy. The Ghost urges that revenge is the prince's only honorable recourse, and young Hamlet agrees. Is there any disturbing note in his accord, any indication that the famous charge of delay is in fact justified? One answer is in the speech that immediately follows the Ghost's exit. The prince reacts with so many and such elaborate words that we might suspect even then that his tongue is readier than his sword.

Question 4. Who says this, and to whom or in what situation: "Frailty, thy name is woman?"

Some students will think this is Polonius or Laertes speaking—a good wrong guess because, as we have just seen, the line does reflect their attitude toward women's sexual nature. How, then, might we recognize the voice as Hamlet's? By its bitter tone and its philosophical cast. Polonius and his son would agree that women are easily led down the garden path, but they are not speaking from a sense of personal betrayal. They are merely warning a girl under their protection against what they think is her own, and all women's, weakness. Both address their words specifically to Ophelia, and they speak in tones ranging from gentleness to scornful condescension. There is none of the vulnerability that Hamlet's words suggest.

This point seems more obvious if students have read carefully enough to recognize the context: Where does Hamlet say this line? It comes halfway through his first soliloquy—a speech, *loquy,* as in *loquacious,* made when a character is *solo,* alone on stage. The Elizabethan convention is that in a soliloquy, a character is speaking aloud his deepest thoughts, and that the audience can therefore accept his words as entirely sincere. When does this first soliloquy occur? It comes just after Hamlet's sarcastic exchange with Claudius—he remains on stage after the king and his court have filed out (I. ii. 129–59). Again, if there is time, I ask someone to read this speech aloud. What is on the prince's mind—what are the feelings behind the public rudeness that he has just shown his new stepfather? Hamlet's mood is bleak: angry, frustrated, suicidally depressed. How does he express this despair? In one hyperbole, one extravagant exaggeration, after another. He wishes that his very flesh would "melt," or that "self-slaughter" had not been forbidden by God. He would welcome either passive or active suicide: Hamlet wants "not to be." This world holds no attraction for him. In direct contrast to the ambitious Polonius, he sees its "uses" as "weary, stale, flat, and unprofitable." He reduces the entire creation to "an unweeded garden," overgrown by "things rank and gross in nature," an ironic reversal of the Eden metaphor. Hamlet is expressing the same conviction that Marcellus will later state on the parapet: The kingdom of Denmark has been ruined, made "rotten." Neither prince nor soldier is yet aware of the cause: the murder of the old king.

What is the reason for Hamlet's black mood? The causes that he cites at first are vague and general, but they come into sharp focus at the first mention of his dead father: "But two months dead! Nay, not so much, not two." Why there? All the emotional ties of his early years have been suddenly and cruelly broken. Not only is his beloved father dead, but his mother has proven fickle. How does Hamlet see her new marriage? Again, his attitude is revealed through his hyperbolic metaphors. Claudius is a "satyr" to old Hamlet's "Hyperion;" Gertrude, a "beast" incapable of real mourning. The bestial image taints even Hamlet's conception of his parents' own marriage, which he had formerly idealized: "Why, she would hang on him/As if increase of *appetite* had grown/By what it *fed* on" (my italics). When Gertrude's "appetite" shifts to his uncle, Hamlet can hardly bear the visions burned into his memory: "Let me not think on't!" he cries. He gives vent to his feelings in the line that this question asks students to identify: "Frailty, thy name is woman." It is a condemnation not merely of his mother but of the whole sex.

As we have noted, the Ghost, too, sees Gertrude and Claudius's love as lust. Has Hamlet merely adopted his dead father's attitude? No. It is important to note where in the play this first soliloquy occurs: before Hamlet is even aware that the Ghost has appeared. Why, then, is he so bitter? His hatred for his uncle is purely instinctive: He has nothing more to accuse Claudius of than passion and ambition. Neither of those faults is sufficient cause for revenge. How does the speech end? "But break my heart, for I must hold my tongue." As both son and subject, Hamlet must obey the new king's will. His powerlessness frustrates him nearly to madness. Hamlet's rage and impotence will be painfully understandable to anyone with a stepparent whom he or she dislikes. It is as the son rather than as the prince that most American adolescents identify with Hamlet, yet many sense that his royal stature enhances his private dilemma. As Hamlet will learn shortly from the Ghost, he not only can but must act to change the odious situation.

Question 5: "He waxes desperate with imagination." Name some point in Act I where Horatio's description of Hamlet's behavior applies.

All the possible answers involve Hamlet's reaction to the Ghost. The first is the episode that provokes Horatio's description: He and Marcellus try to prevent Hamlet from following the beckoning spirit (I. iv.). Hamlet, nearly hysterical, exclaims, "My fate cries out," fights off his well-meaning friends, and rushes after the apparition. Why do Horatio and Marcellus try to restrain Hamlet? They are afraid for him, but on what basis? Horatio warns the prince that the Ghost might be a malevolent force, that it might "tempt" him to some perilous place. Worse, he cautions, it might assume a "horrible form" that would "deprive [Hamlet's] sovereignty of reason/And draw [him] into madness." Hamlet's response is to defy his friends, in a way that shows the first symptoms of waxing desperate with imagination.

A more striking example occurs just after the Ghost has spoken to Hamlet (I. v.). What is Hamlet told? The whole story of his uncle's treachery and his father's suffering. What is the effect of this news? At the Ghost's departure, Hamlet is left in a state of shock. Frantic, he calls for help to heaven, earth, even hell. He is on the verge of physical collapse. He tries to rally the forces of his own body, calling on his heart not to break and his "sinews" not to buckle—in plain language, he is afraid that he is going to faint. Are there other signs of his distraction? His mental powers are scattered—he describes his head as a "distracted globe." His actions are erratic. He curses Claudius, snatches his journal to jot down a commonplace event that he has just seen in a mad new light, repeats himself, swears and exclaims. Only the recollection of the Ghost's final injunction, "Remember me," restores Hamlet to a semblance of self-control.

But when his friends enter, seeking him, his mood again becomes overexcited, almost frantic. Hamlet's attitude toward his worried fellows is completely inappropriate to the situation. He is playful, sly, evasive. The puzzled Horatio calls his responses to their anxious questions "wild and whirling words." The mild reproach is meant to recall Hamlet to himself. Does it work? Hamlet is too wound up to heed it. He insists, repeatedly and excitedly, that his friends swear to reveal nothing of what they have seen. Suddenly the Ghost echoes Hamlet's urgings from under the stage. What is the prince's reaction? Hamlet, who has been a model of courtesy and reverence toward his father, hails his spirit with jovial irreverence. He uses the familiar "thou," and calls old Hamlet by a series of pet names: "boy," "truepenny," "old mole." Even Shakespeare himself joins for a moment in this mockery: The Ghost again demands that the men "swear," and Hamlet says lightly, "Come on! You hear this fellow in the cellarage. Consent to swear." The "fellow in the cellarage" is literally the actor under the stage calling out his ghostly lines. The playwright risks breaking the mood by calling attention to the conventions of his own theater. Does this joking destroy the dramatic illusion? No, instead it suggests how close Hamlet is to losing his grip. The presence of his father's spirit drives him to gallows humor and frantic mood swings.

Does the scene end with the hero still out of control? He finally calms down enough to warn Horatio and Marcellus that he may in the future choose "To put an antic disposition on." What does this key line mean? That Hamlet may feign the very mood we have just seen him display in earnest. This brings us to a major question of the play: Is Hamlet mad? Yes and no. Here, for example, he is wildly excited, even hysterical, but certainly not subject to delusions, paranoid convictions of persecution or of grandeur. It is not so much Hamlet as his world that has gone insane. As the scene ends, his reason reasserts itself. He addresses the Ghost with touching concern: "Rest, rest, perturbed spirit!" He reluctantly accepts his mission of revenge. What do Hamlet's last lines mean? The "distracted globe" is back in its proper orbit;

now it is "the time" that is "out of joint." Hamlet feels sufficiently in control to vow to "set it right."

Bonus question: Name two potential conflicts that Act I introduces. Put the answer in the form of _____ vs. _____.

This is an easy question because there are so many possible answers. Even people who have only skimmed the act should get the answer right. The question is worth asking because it forces students to think about the play's structure. Three types of answers are possible. The largest conflict is that between kingdoms: Denmark vs. Norway. The most frequent clash is that between characters: Hamlet vs. Claudius, Hamlet vs. Gertrude, Hamlet vs. Polonius, Hamlet vs. Ophelia. What does this list suggest? The troubled prince is clearly the main character: He is at the center of every important opposition of wills. What about Polonius vs. Ophelia, someone may ask. That answer would not get full credit; the key is the word "potential." When Polonius opposes Ophelia's will, she accedes to his wishes with only a mild show of protest. That conflict is resolved almost as soon as it begins. The third sort of conflict is that within Hamlet: suicide vs. life, duty to revenge vs. scruples against murder, ideal vs. actual behavior, talking vs. taking action. To which dramatic techniques does this question refer? Contrast and juxtaposition—Shakespeare both implies the nature of the hero and moves the plot forward by putting characters and issues in opposition. He shows rather than tells what Hamlet is like and what forces, external and internal, the prince is up against.

While, on the surface, all these questions are factual, most involve interpretation as well. The last two questions, in particular, demand that students use their ingenuity. Many will be pleasantly surprised at their success in answering the quiz questions. But the benefits go beyond helping students to understand a particular act. The implication of an open-ended question is that *Hamlet*, like any great book, is multilayered and capable of many interpretations, including some that the "expert" teacher may not have thought of. Asking students to express their own interpretations, and to listen to those of their classmates, confirms that idea and gives the students a surer sense of what to read for in the next act. In other words, the quiz should be both a test of what students have read and a means of teaching them how to read.

Chapter 4

Mime as Meaning: *Hamlet*

Preliminary Exercise: The Telling Emotion

Not all students are able to express their understanding of a play in words, so I appeal to the actor in them. First, to get everyone energized, I use a simple warm-up exercise: to mime a particular emotion. It helps to do this early on, both to vary the usual discussion format and to overcome inhibitions. Some time during the study of Act I of *Hamlet*—for example, the day after the first quiz—I ask the class to stand and form a circle at the front of the room. (If the classroom is small, they may have to surround the desks or move to a larger space like the auditorium or the gym.) Then, I tell them to stay in the circle but turn to face the back of the next student, and to start walking. As they walk, I clap or pound the desk in a steady rhythm. Then I call out a feeling expressed by one or more of the characters in the first act of *Hamlet*—for example, "suspicion." As soon as they hear the word, the students are to begin silently acting out that emotion, with the clap or the beat to keep them moving. After a few turns around the circle, I say, "Stop!" They pause, turn back toward the center of the circle, and mime suspicion in one frozen pose. Only then do they get to look around at what their fellow mimes are doing.

Next, I split the circle in two, and call out a second emotion—for example, "terror." The two halves of the group alternate as silent actors and audience. Before the mimes relax, I add a new component: I ask the audience to describe what they see. What are the actors doing to show terror? In one class, for example, a boy was grimacing in a silent scream, mouth wide open, hands raised like helpless claws. A girl was cringing, hiding her face with her hands; another was squatting, one eye peeping over her tense fingers. Another boy was frozen in mid-run, looking back over his shoulder and calling silently for help. A girl was standing stock still, hand on her heart, eyes raised, jaw dropped.

Afterwards, we talk about what we have just seen: What kinds of experiences could prompt such fear? Do these statues have any similarities? What—if anything—can they teach us about the characters in the first act of *Hamlet*? Someone will probably say that they all look like they've seen a ghost. Modern audiences don't believe in ghosts—or do they? What do we have in common with Marcellus, Bernardo, and Hamlet himself, in the scene where *they* see one? Most of us dislike darkness and winter cold and unexplained phenomena. As mystery novels and horror movies continue to make clear, ghosts suddenly appearing at midnight still "harrow" not just Horatio but most of us with "fear and wonder."

After the audience has finished commenting, I turn to the actors and ask: What happens to our bodies when we feel afraid? Someone will probably say that we feel alone, or small, or helpless. We want to cry out for help, or hide, or both. One girl said that at first she couldn't get into the mood. What changed that? Imagining her grandmother's basement, a place she'd been afraid of as a little girl because it smelled musty and because she'd once seen a huge spider there. A third said that as soon as he began forming his mouth into a scream, he felt his stomach contract and his hands begin to sweat; having to stay silent made it seem even more frightening, like not being able to cry out in a nightmare.

After the actors have described their feelings, I ask the audience to comment on their own responses. Someone noted that all these actors were either shrinking or trying to get away. Several of them looked incredulous—this cannot be happening, their expressions said. Another said that as soon as he saw the actor glancing over his shoulder as he "ran," he remembered a time that the class bully was chasing him, and he felt a rush of adrenalin. So for both actor and audience, physical associations, with gestures or facial expressions or postures, can be the key to understanding a character.

The aim of this technique is not only to teach students something about a particular episode in *Hamlet* but to recreate the experience of being in a theater. The objective is to make the students react as actors and spectators, rather than as passive readers. This technique, a common kind of warm-up for actors, can be used with students of any age and level of ability. I once participated in a version of it—on random emotions, not related to any particular play—at a summer institute for teachers run by Shakespeare & Company. Our group ranged in age from late twenties to early sixties, and in experience from people who had never set foot on a stage to veteran actors and directors. For us, too, it inspired camaraderie and a release of creative energy.

If time permits, I go on to mimes of other emotions: "depression" (to help students sense Hamlet's mood), "triumph" or "guilt" (for Claudius), "timidity" (for Ophelia), "self-righteousness" (for Polonius). I do not make these connections explicit: The mime is meant to be based on real-life experience. With younger or less able students, I might also do mime of a role, such as "king" or "daughter" or "father."

These exercises can also serve as an audition: They allow me to note which students are imaginative or agile or uninhibited, and to see how they project their feelings "on stage." The most promising actors, in class as on Broadway, are often not the scholarly types. Even during simple mimes, talented performers can illuminate moments in a play and win some heartening applause. Later in the term, I often find that the same students also excel at more complicated acting tasks.

The Two Faces of Claudius

By the end of Act I, students should have come to the same conclusion as Hamlet himself: Claudius has more than one face. He is both king and murderer, charismatic leader and hypocrite. A class that was having trouble understanding those seeming contradictions inspired me to invent a more involved mime exercise: "The Two Faces of Claudius." It works like this: I ask for six volunteers to walk to the front of the class and pair up. "All right, which of you is A?" I ask.

"What? What do you mean?"

Without explaining, I say, "A's, will each of you raise your right hand?"

After a few shrugs, the hands go up.

"Each of you is Claudius's public face, the side he shows to his court. All right, B's, raise your hands. You're his private face, the self he becomes when he's in his own chamber. Remember, you're two sides of the same man, so you have to be linked somehow."

A girl asks: "Is anyone else there, like Gertrude or Hamlet?"

"No, the king is alone. But he might be thinking about one of them."

"Can we move?"

"This is supposed to be a statue, but you may make one repeated movement if you want to, like a mechanical toy. Okay, you have two minutes to work this out. Don't just talk. Use your whole body. Try out some poses and expressions, and see if they change when you link up. When I say, 'Stop,' freeze and show us your two 'faces.'"

I distract the rest of the class with a discussion on some related issue but not the process going on in front of the room. After a few self-conscious moments, the Siamese statues start forming. I give them a while to experiment. Then, once the poses are fairly set, I ask them to freeze.

In one class, a pair showed a tall, athletic boy assuming the confident stance of the conqueror, head back, arms folded, back straight; but at his side, crouching and clutching his belt, was a cringing girl. In contrast to the condescending glance of A was B's thumb-chewing look of terror. Face A took one step forward in an attempt to shake off face B, but the cringing figure clung on and crawled after.

The next pair, both girls, were sitting in back-to-back chairs, their sides to the class. A was nodding and smiling serenely, the right hand raised in a benevolent gesture; B was grimacing fiercely and looking around suspiciously, the left hand raised to ward off blows. Here the repeated gesture was the turning head—A to bestow blessings on the court, B to search every corner for traitors.

The last statue had A holding an imaginary crown just above his head; he was facing the audience and his expression was proud and triumphant. The B figure, meanwhile, had turned away, his back touching A's side at a three-quarter angle. He, too, was holding an imaginary crown, but clutching it tightly to his chest, his shoulders hunched and his expression wary. Neither figure moved.

I asked the rest of the class to walk up to the three pairs and observe—to be the visitors to the sculpture gallery. After a round of applause, I asked the audience to describe what they saw: What impressions of Claudius did they get? Did the three versions have anything in common? What new insights did the statues give them about Claudius's strengths and weaknesses? Someone who had felt only Claudius's ruthlessness before might notice the fear that his transgressions could provoke. Another might see the competence of the man, the splendid public figure that he makes. Some might question for the first time how much of his private self he reveals to his new queen.

After the audience has commented, the actors can talk about how they felt. What difference did it make to be representing only half of the man? Did they change a gesture or a concept in response to their partner? Did they discuss the change, or simply do it? Would they change anything now, after seeing the other pairs? They might mention the effects of ensemble playing, of how a conception grows in relation to other actors. They might realize the range of choices possible in playing Claudius—and some of the pleasures of making such choices. They might comment on how playing a role makes you more sensitive to other actors' choices. The older and the more articulate the class, the more they will notice. I do not, of course, expect the acting to be of professional calibre. Some students will be self-conscious or melodramatic or wooden. But others will give deeply felt and inventive performances. The audience, having tried the exercise and realized its demands, is in a better position to appreciate those efforts. Their comments, on these scenes and on more polished performances that the class sees later, tend to be both informed and warm.

The Two Faces technique can work with any conflicted character—with Ophelia in her madness, with Laertes in his vengeful stage, with Hamlet in nearly every act. It is equally useful for other plays—in bringing out Iago's hypocrisy, for example, or Viola's concealed attraction to Duke Orsino, or Lady Macbeth's ambivalence about murdering the fatherly Duncan. This method gets students on their feet and spotlights people who are better actors than readers. It creates some odd couples and encourages them to communicate and cooperate. It gives a class's response to the play an immediacy that reading and discussion may not provide. Finally, the mime becomes both a reward and a summary for the study of the text that has led to this felt understanding.

Chapter 5

The Live Sculpture: *Hamlet*

A more complex mime exercise than the Two Faces technique is one that I learned from Mary King Austin at the Shakespeare & Company summer institute: the Live Sculpture. The object is to create a silent arrangement of some key moment in a play—the balcony scene in *Romeo and Juliet*, the blinding of Gloucester in *King Lear*, the murder of Desdemona in *Othello*. The goal is not a literal re-creation of the episode but a grouping that suggests what each character knows and feels, and how he or she relates to the others. It may include not only characters literally present in the scene but any who exert an influence. For example, the senior Capulets and Montagues could be shown blocking the lovers' attempts to reach one another; Iago might be hovering over and laughing at Desdemona's death struggle. The sculpture may even include a character who never appears in the play—the Duchess of Gloucester reacting to her husband's illegitimate son; the Nurse's dead daughter, whose place in the woman's affections Juliet fills. What this technique asks students to do is to look at a scene with a director's eye and then show, not tell, the subtext: what is beneath and beyond the words. Here is how it works.

When I want a change from the usual reading-writing-discussion format or when I sense that some people are having trouble understanding motives and relationships, I tell the class that we're going to do something completely different. At this point in our study of *Hamlet*, for example, I want students to understand not only the conflicting feelings in Claudius but also how they affect his relationships with his family and his subjects. I say that we're going to create a live sculpture of the king's first public audience. I ask someone to volunteer to be the "sculptor." His job, I explain, is to choose classmates who will act as the various statues, and to arrange them in poses that show their roles in the scene and their relationships to one another. He may describe how he wants someone to stand, or, briefly, what he thinks the character may be feeling at this moment. But the emphasis should be on practice, not theory. I ask the sculptor to pick and arrange the statues one at a time, in what seems to him their order of importance. He may limit the choices to the major actors in the scene or he may add minor players. He may also include a character who is not, in fact, present but who influences the action at this point—someone who is on a journey or who has died, for example.

Even with these instructions, there is often a flurry of questions—Can girls play male characters? What if someone does not want to be in a scene? Can the actors move? Can they use props? What if the sculptor gets things wrong? I try to dispose of such questions quickly, before the energy gets lost in self-consciousness: Girls may be cast as males, and vice versa. Everyone has to take part. Each actor is allowed one movement, clockwork-style, as in the Two Faces exercise. "Props" should be imaginary, suggested by gestures, but actors may use a piece of furniture, like a chair, if it is important to the scene. If the sculptor misreads a relationship or an action or leaves out something crucial, there will be two chances to correct it. Once the group sculpture is complete, each actor will be allowed to move, to create her or his own statue. Finally, the audience and then the "statues" will be asked to comment, both on the individual figures and on the ensemble.

On this occasion, Holly, who has been in several school musicals, volunteers to be the sculptor. She looks around the class and finally picks Clint, a tall, handsome boy. "You're Claudius," she says. He blushes, but follows her good-humoredly to the front of the class. "Could you help me move Ms. H's desk chair to the middle of the room?" They put it in the center of the "stage." "Okay, that's your throne. Sit in it, and for right now just look pleased with yourself and in charge." He sits. "No, sit up more. Pretend you're holding one of those sticks kings always have." "A scepter," someone volunteers. "Yeah," she says. She squints at him critically. "Put your chin up a little more. This is your big moment, like Christmas morning and graduation all at once." He draws himself up straighter.

"Good. Okay, now I need Gertrude." She looks the class over again and points to Molly, a large, bold-looking girl, who gives a pleased giggle. "Now we need another throne, a smaller one. Are there any more chairs? No, we'll just have to use a desk. Tom, can I borrow yours? Thanks." They move it to the right of Claudius's. "Now, sit down, Gertrude, and look at Claudius. You're in love, and you're really glad to be queen again." The girl tries a Madonna come-hither look. "Not *that* much in love. The whole court is there, don't forget."

Molly looks offended. "Where? I don't see anyone."

"Just pretend. No, wait, let's get 'em up here. Who else is around?" She appeals to me. "Can I look in my book?"

"No, no books," I say, "but you can get help from your audience."

"Help me, you guys," Holly pleads, and people begin speaking up.

"It said 'courtiers' in the book. I looked it up—people who hang around the court."

"Yeah, and the old guy—Polonius is there."

"And his son. What's his name?"

The sculptor's memory has been jogged. "Right, Laertes. Okay." She goes up to a thin blond boy. "Ken, you're Laertes. Come on up and stand to the king's left. He's just given you permission to go back to France, so you like him a lot. Bow a little in his direction. Yeah, that's it. Now, let's see," she looks at a heavy-set boy and nods. "Mike, you're Polonius. Come and stand next to Laertes, and put one hand on his shoulder. You're really proud of your boy and glad that the king appreciates him, too, but you hate to let him go. Look a little more sad." Mike wrinkles his forehead. "Can you look older, too?"

He bends over, and leans on a imaginary cane. "How's this?"

"Great!" She stands back. "Wow, this is practically all men. We oughta have some court ladies here, too. Let's see, Amy and Laura, will you come up here? Get over there with Polonius and Laertes. Bill, stand next to Laura, and Jim, next to Amy, and take their arms. Okay, you ladies have fans, and you're staring straight at the royals. Naw, this looks lopsided. Could we have one couple move over beside Gertrude? Bill and Laura—yeah, good."

"How are we supposed to feel? Do we suspect anything?" Amy asks.

"Hmmm. Good question. *You* do, you're looking a little suspicious, but the other three are just going along with it—the yes-men. Hide behind your fan a little and stare at Claudius. Good... So, that's it, I guess."

"Hey, what about Hamlet?"

"Oh, wow, how could I forget *him*? He's the one who changes everything." Her eyes skim the class and stop at a sallow-faced boy with a wry expression. "Jeremy, you're Hamlet." He starts, then follows her to the front. "Okay, you're right at the front, looking out at us. No, not in the center, off to the right. That's it. Now look back over your shoulder at Claudius and Gertrude, but at us, too."

"Huh? How can I do both of those things?"

"Well, stand at an angle. Yeah, point your shoulder at them but look at us. Okay, now cross your arms. You're *not* going to go along with celebration stuff."

She gives the panorama a last critical glance. "Gertrude, you have one hand on Claudius's arm, but you're looking at Hamlet. And you're worried. Okay, that's it. I'm done."

Now I ask the audience to look carefully at the sculpture, standing up and walking around it if necessary. After everyone has seen it, I ask for a round of applause. Next, I tell Holly to go up to each actor, in the order in which she chose them, and ask if they want to move. Claudius says that he likes the triumphant pose for *one* moment, but wants to be able to check Hamlet out—to turn his head and glare at him—no, just shift his gaze and narrow his eyes. When he does that, Gertrude decides to turn and look at him, questioningly, and her grip on his arm tightens. As they shift, Hamlet does, too: He puts his hands on his hips and turns to confront them directly. The courtiers react by looking more suspiciously at Hamlet. Only Laertes remains smiling and oblivious. Finally, Polonius says that he feels he should be between the king and Hamlet, bowing and holding a hand out to each. The actors decide not to switch back and forth between the two poses but to hold the second. The class claps again.

I tell the actors to relax but to stay in their places. Then I ask them to comment on their choices.

Clint, a.k.a. Claudius, says, "As soon as Hol added Hamlet to the scene, I felt threatened. I mean, I know that I killed his father, and I'm afraid he does, too."

Molly-Gertrude responds, "As soon as Clint got defensive, I felt worried. I don't want to know what happened to my first husband, but I think I *do*—at least, on some level."

Bill—a courtier—says, "I think the courtiers know, too. That's why I looked daggers at Hamlet. I think we're all Claudius's boys: if he goes, we do, too."

Jeremy-Hamlet objects: "But Hamlet doesn't know about the murder yet, does he? Has he met the ghost yet or not?"

Clint: "He hasn't, but he already hates his uncle. He's going to make a big public scene and embarrass him, remember."

Me: "So we definitely need Hamlet there. Does everyone agree that all three members of the Hamlet family suspect that something is rotten?"

Nods and mumbles. From a girl in the corner: "Yeah. I liked the second sculpture better, 'cause it showed that."

Clint: "I actually liked the first version better, because it showed the image we were trying to get people to accept—the new king, the new marriage, everything A-okay."

Holly: "Maybe I should've done both poses—you know, the surface and the real thing."

Several murmurs of approval.

Me: "Okay. Was there any statue that *didn't* seem right?"

Laura: "Well, I'm not sure that Polonius would be exactly torn between Claudius and Hamlet. I think he's the king's man, whoever that king is. I'd have him lean more toward Clint."

Mike-Polonius concedes.

Me: "Is anyone missing, anyone you would add?"

Ken, who played Laertes, sits up: "What about Ophelia? She was there, wasn't she?"

Several students check their books. Meg says, "It doesn't list her—I mean, she doesn't talk in this scene—but it does include the whole court. And if her father and brother are there, she'd have to be."

Me: "Good. Be Ophelia for a minute, Meg. What would you do?"

Meg stands up. "Can I get Ken and Jeremy back up here? Okay, I'd just stand there and look back and forth between them."

"Try it. What do you think, people?"

Holly: "She needs Polonius there, too. She's such a Daddy's girl."

"Okay, Mike, back up for a second. How do you feel now, Meg?"

"Oh, like he's watching me—or I should be watching him. I think I'd look back and forth between him and Hamlet. But I'm really happy right now. Clueless."

"Do it. What do you think, audience?"

Molly: "Yeah, that's good. It's easy to forget about Ophelia, but she's going to be destroyed by all this stuff she doesn't even suspect right now. Poor thing."

Me: "So, is that it?"

Jeremy: "No, I think that my old dad should be there—his ghost, I mean."

Ken: "But he hasn't even met Hamlet yet."

Jeremy: "So? He's what's really behind this whole scene."

Me: "Okay, Jeremy, cast him."

Jeremy: "Dave. Drag that desk over behind the throne. Okay, stand up on it and sort of hover over Claudius."

Dave: "Should I, like, stab him?"

Jeremy: "No. That's Hamlet's job. But you can point to him—yeah—and sort of beckon to Hamlet."

Holly: "Ooh, wow, wish I'd thought of that."

Me: "Good work, everybody. Okay, let's do the whole sculpture one more time, with Ophelia and the Ghost added."

Holly: "Can people switch back and forth between the two poses—the glitzy surface and the ugly stuff underneath?"

Me: "You're the boss."

Holly: "Okay. I want the two poses, but the Ghost will only be in the second one. Dave, crouch down behind the throne. Now when he climbs up and looms over Claudius, everyone else switch to the guilty pose."

This time the switch in mood is striking and the applause enthusiastic.

If there is time, and the interest has remained high, I ask the class to do a second sculpture during the same period. Another scene from Act I that works well is Laertes's farewell to his father and sister. There, too, the tasks are to decide how close to make the family members, how much to reveal about their hidden feelings. This assignment can also be useful for a mid-play climax: the terrified exit of Claudius from Hamlet's "Mousetrap," the murder of Banquo in *Macbeth*, the public shaming of Hero in *Much Ado About Nothing*, the "trial" of Goneril and Regan in *King Lear*, the confrontation of Antony and Augustus Caesar in *Antony and Cleopatra*. It works equally well for a final panorama—the "quarry" of deaths in the last scene of *Hamlet* and *Lear*, the marriage dances at the end of *As You Like It* and *Much Ado About Nothing*, the recognitions and revelations that close *Twelfth Night* and *The Winter's Tale*. Finally, I have used it with not a particular scene but a general relationship—e.g., the evil sisters' battle for the bastard Edmund's affections in *King Lear*, or Iago's taunting of Othello, both of which continue through several scenes.

The group sculptures usually become more inventive as the semester goes on. As students come to understand the goals of the assignment and get to know one another better, they are usually more willing to risk looking silly or melodramatic. The performances become more intense and the sculptors' focus sharper.

Like the Two Faces exercise, the Live Sculpture serves several purposes, and it works for students of every ability level. It rewards daring, spontaneity, and instinct, the nonverbal qualities that fine actors share. It also clarifies the director's role, by reducing casting and blocking to the simplest terms and by showing how a single change in expression or position creates a ripple effect in every actor. Whether students are directing, playing in, or watching such silent scenes, this technique can build confidence in those who do not see themselves as scholars. At the same time, it calls on the critical gifts of students who are not natural actors but can hear and explain a nuance of meaning. Both kinds of students learn a new appreciation of their peers; a talented few make the heady discovery that they can act or direct or analyze with equal ease. As in playing on a winning team, cooperation, not competition, becomes the ruling principle, and everyone gets a chance at the fun of seeing a play or the thrill of performing before an audience. In other words, the Live Sculpture serves theater's essential communal role in a classroom setting.

Chapter 6

Speaking the Speech:
The Sonnet and the
Dramatic Monologue—
Antony and Cleopatra

For years, I have asked students to memorize a sonnet or a passage from whatever play we were studying. But I always required that they write down the memorized passage—until the semester when I had a dyslexic and an ESL student in the same class. Both claimed that they found it much easier to recite a memorized speech. When I took them at their word, I discovered a simple principle: It is hard to say something that you don't understand, particularly if you are speaking to someone else. Although not everyone has the skill or the nerve to speak the speech trippingly on the tongue, as Hamlet advised, saying it makes most people more alert to the meanings of words and to shifts in rhythm and tone.

For a monologue, knowing the context, both in the play as a whole and in the character's experience, gives the actor a sense of the feelings being expressed. In a sonnet, that information is implied: Each one is like a playlet, with the plot and the relationship between speaker and unseen addressee ready to be discovered. To keep the experience fresh, I prefer to avoid the best-known sonnets—e.g., "My mistress' eyes" and "Let me not to the marriage of true minds." Whatever the student's choice, the basis for it should be some intuitive connection with the piece, not ease of memorizing already familiar lines.

A Sample Assignment

I begin by giving students a list of eight or so passages to choose from. I allow two or three days for memorization—in acting parlance, for getting "off book"—either over a weekend or during a light homework time. Each class starts with a short voice and movement warm-up: Everyone stands in a circle. A volunteer makes a simple movement—a bow; a step

43

forward, hand thrust out; a twirl—and everyone in the circle imitates it in chorus. Then it is the next person's turn to initiate a movement. The exercise continues until everyone in the circle has begun a movement. The second kind of exercise involves sound, first an inarticulate one—a grunt, a giggle, a squeal. Next comes a word or a phrase, preferably a quotation from the passage—"O, Antony" or "outcast state." Again, each student says one and everyone echoes it simultaneously.

These warm-ups serve several purposes: to get people's sluggish blood moving—to generate the energy that acting takes; to increase rapport, since it's easier to perform for an audience you trust; and to make people relax. Inevitably, there are funny moments—a cracked voice, a clumsy gesture or split seam, a silly sound. The laughter can be a release for tension and a source of camaraderie.

The Performance

We perform right in the classroom—in fact, that familiar setting is usually preferable to the big auditorium. One area of the room is designated as "the stage." The actors themselves determine the order of the performances. A student who feels ready seizes the spotlight by standing up and walking to the stage area. She asks someone to act as prompter. If the actor says "line," the prompter reads the whole line in a neutral voice and the actor repeats it with feeling. For the novice, remembering lines in the presence of an audience may seem like the main challenge. I stress that memorization is only *one* requirement here, and not the major one. Once the feeling is clear, once the actor and the character have merged, the speaker will want to say the lines. Not knowing them will be more frustrating than threatening. Memorization will become a necessary but preliminary goal, like getting in shape before a game.

The actor takes a few minutes to set the scene with any furniture or props he might want, to establish eye contact with his audience, and to take some deep breaths. He will perform at least twice. The first time is the "rough draft": he gets through the lines, charging them with what feeling he can. My one firm requirement is that the audience listen respectfully and, afterwards, applaud. Then the discussion begins, with me asking two questions, first of the actor and then of the audience: Where is the performance now—what is coming through? Where should it go? To show how this technique works, I will describe four examples from actual classes, two on the sonnets and two on monologues from *Antony and Cleopatra*.

The Sonnet

Rob spoke Sonnet 29, "When in Disgrace with Fortune and Men's Eyes":

When, in disgrace with fortune and men's eyes,
I all alone beweep my outcast state,
And trouble deaf heaven with my bootless cries,
And look upon myself and curse my fate,
Wishing me like to one more rich in hope,
Featur'd like him, like him with friends possess'd,
Desiring this man's art, and that man's scope,
With what I most enjoy contented least;
Yet in these thoughts myself almost despising,
Haply I think on thee, and then my state
(Like to the lark at break of day arising
From sullen earth) sings hymns at heaven's gate;
   For thy sweet love remember'd such wealth brings,
   That then I scorn to change my state with kings.

Afterwards, Rob said that his voice seemed flat, that the whole poem came out in a monotone. The class did not agree: Several people told Rob the opening lines sounded convincingly despairing. "That's the part I know," he responded. "Up to the 'yet,' I feel pretty good about the memorization."

Me: "Where are you now—what are you feeling as you say those first lines?"

"Well, that everyone else is better off than he is. He's sort of jealous."

"Of what? What are the most painful words?"

"He feels in *disgrace*—that's painful. 'With what I most enjoy contented least'—that's about as depressed as you can get."

"What would be an example of that for you?"

"For me? Well, like if I didn't even want to play computer games or read my *Far Side* books. That would be depressed."

"Do you see any other signs that the speaker is depressed?"

A shrug and silence from Rob. Josh offers: "He's alone, and he's crying, at the beginning anyway."

Rob: "He is?"

Josh: "He says, 'I all alone beweep my outcast state.' "

"Oh, wow. I missed that."

"Are there any other words that you don't understand?"

"Well, what does 'bootless' mean?"

Karen, who also chose this sonnet, says, "I looked it up—it means 'futile,' 'useless.' "

Rob: "Oh, so crying doesn't do any good."

"Try just that line: 'And trouble deaf heaven with my bootless cries.' Stress the strong words."

This time it comes out with the accent on "deaf" and "bootless cries"; the tone sounds frustrated and despairing. The class murmurs approval.

Me: "Good, Rob. But right now you're pretty much a talking head. How can you act out your feelings?"

"Maybe I should be sitting down."

"Okay, try it. Any other ideas?"

Sarah: "I think it would help if he talked to us—maybe pointed to us when he mentions the friends he's jealous of."

Chuckles from the class, sheepish grin from Rob. He sits down, puts his hand to his forehead, lowers his eyes. At "trouble deaf heaven," he looks up to the ceiling, ends the quatrain staring straight ahead, pounding fist into open palm at "curse my fate." When he starts his series of envious wishes, he goes up on his lines and has to be prompted. But the despair and the envy come through, as several people assure him. Rob, however, is disappointed. "I knew those lines before," he says.

"Actually, forgetting your lines is a good sign. It means you're getting away from just saying words and into really feeling them. Your head isn't working as well—your gut and heart are interfering. The goal is for all of them to be working together. If that doesn't happen, you may sound letter-perfect but phony—you'll be acting a part, not merging yourself with the character. So forgetting lines is an important step."

To the class: "Now which part of Rob's performance is working best?"

Mike: "I like the first half—I can really feel the despair. But the second part sounds kind of stiff."

"Rob, do you feel that the tone should shift at some point?"

"Yeah—at 'Haply I think on thee.' Does 'haply' mean 'happily'?"

"No—by chance, luck. We still use that meaning in the word 'happen.' But it's also a pun here, I think."

"Yeah, because suddenly he *is* happy."

"Try saying 'I' instead of 'he.' "

Rob grins, an agreement to play this latest game.

"What changes your mood?"

"I remember that I'm in love—or that I've been in love."

"Which is it?"

"I can't tell. 'Thy sweet love rememb'red'—am I remembering something that's over or remembering that I've still got the love? Or maybe it's not that kind of thing at all. Maybe it's a friend or one of my parents that I'm thinking of. Does it make any difference?"

"It does to *you*. Those lines are ambiguous. Which are the stronger choices for you?"

"Well, I don't really think it's Dave or my mom I'm thinking of. I think it's a girl. And I'd rather be in love now, but I feel like this guy is older than me and the love is over. Maybe even that she's dead."

"Which words give you those feelings?"

"Let's see—it's 'sweet love' and it makes him want to 'sing hymns at heaven's gate.' There's something sad about that."

"Okay, how can you get that feeling through to us? Do you want to have someone play the lover so you can say the last lines to her?"

"No. I think it's in the past. Why don't I just look at that poster of Emily Brontë?"

"Okay, try it. One more thing: What are you feeling by the end?"

"I'm actually pretty high—I mean, I'm 'arising/From sullen earth'."

"You are? That makes you sound like Superman."

"Okay, not all of me. But my 'state' is—does that mean my mood? I remember her and then I suddenly feel great."

"Does that suggest a movement for you to make?"

"Oh, I should stand up. And maybe look up to heaven again, but happily this time."

"Try it."

This time both the despair and the exhilaration come through. Rob still has trouble remembering and getting feeling into a few of the lines. The couplet is a special problem: with the last words, his pace sped up and his voice trailed off.

"What are the key words in those last two lines?"

" 'Scorn' and 'kings'?"

"Right. How about 'state,' too? How many times does that word appear?"

"Oh, wow. First, there's 'outcast state.' Then he remembers the 'sweet love' and his 'state' flies up to heaven's gate and starts singing. And finally he wouldn't trade his 'state' even for a king's."

"Good. Say just the couplet, and make those feelings come through."

This time the warmth of 'thy sweet love' and the pride and triumph of 'scorn' and 'kings' ring in the room.

Sonnet 71, which Sarah chose, follows a different pattern—not octave and sestet, with the change in mood heightened in the couplet, but three quatrains, with the couplet as final confirmation of their message:

No longer mourn for me when I am dead
Than you shall hear the surly sullen bell
Give warning to the world that I am fled
From this vile world with vilest worms to dwell.
Nay, if you read this line, remember not
The hand that writ it; for I love you so
That I in your sweet thoughts would be forgot,
If thinking on me then should make you woe.
O, if (I say) you look upon this verse
When I (perhaps) compounded am with clay,
Do not so much as my poor name rehearse,
But let your love even with my life decay;
*   Lest the wise world should look into your moan*
*   And mock you with me after I am gone.*

Sarah's delivery is clear but monotonous, and her pace speeds up as she goes on. This time the problem is not with the literal meaning: Footnotes make clear that "bell" refers to that passing bell rung once to commemorate each year of the dead person's life and that "compounded" means mixed with earth, as the body is after burial. The problem is gauging the sonnet's tone. Sarah senses that something is going wrong: "I'm having trouble because it all sounds alike to me. The speaker gives—I give—the whole message in the first line: Don't mourn for me."

"Why not? Why don't you want your lover to grieve over your death?"

"I don't want him to be sad—'If thinking on me then should make you woe.'"

"Is there anything in the poem that contradicts that?"

Puzzled silence from Sarah. David offers, "Well, this guy has a pretty morbid imagination."

"What do you mean?"

"All those descriptions of decay. 'Vilest worms'—that's pretty disgusting. He's sort of rubbing it in that he'll be rotting in the grave."

Sarah: "He? I thought the speaker was a woman."

David: "What do you mean? Shakespeare wrote it."

Sarah: "The author's not the speaker. Anyway, it works just as well for a woman, and I'm saying it."

Me: "Sarah's right. Most of the sonnets work for either gender. They're easier to understand if you can read them through your own eyes. Okay, is there any other motive that *she* has for not wanting her lover to mourn?"

"Yes. Look at the couplet. She thinks other people will laugh at him if he does."

"Why?"

"I don't know. Maybe because she's not worth mourning for? Like, maybe she's ugly or old or already married."

"Which reason works best for you?"

"I like 'old'. I think the lover is younger and more innocent."

David: "Or maybe it's just that mourning for someone makes you weak. Other people could laugh at you for laying your feelings open like that."

Sarah: "That's a pretty cynical thought."

David: "I think this—person—is pretty cynical."

Me: "About what? Sarah, what are the two enemies to love here?"

"Well, time—it causes death and decay. And other people who don't sympathize—the 'wise world'."

"Good. What's the tone of those last lines?"

"It's pretty sarcastic—snide."

"Okay, let's go for sad and morbid at first, then sarcastic and snide. Do you want to stand this time?"

"No, I'm going to try sitting. I think I'll be writing this time—writing 'this verse'."

"Okay, do you want someone to speak these lines to?"

"Maybe I should. Okay—Bill." She picks a fresh-faced boy, younger looking than most people in the class. Sarah arranges a desk for herself and another for Bill. She turns hers toward Bill's and his so that it is facing the class. She begins by looking down, holding an imaginary pen and writing, then up at 'surly sullen bell', down again at 'read this line'. At 'love you so', she reaches a hand toward his cheek. At 'wise world', she gives us an arch look. This time both the sarcasm and the feeling that it conceals—real anguish at the thought of death—come through movingly.

The Monologue

Unlike a sonnet, a monologue is not self-contained. How can the actor recall, and suggest to the audience, the larger context, the speaker's situation and attitude at this point in the play? It helps to ask the same kinds of questions that came up in the performance of the poem: Where are you at this moment, literally and emotionally? What do you want? What are you feeling? Are there shifts in your tone? Are there points at which an action is implied?

After studying *Antony and Cleopatra*, I asked students to choose one of eight monologues, four for men and four for women (line numbers are from the Pelican edition):

For men:
1. Antony, I. ii. 173–88
2. Caesar, I. iv. 57–71
3. Enobarbus, II. ii. 192–206
4. Antony, IV. xiv. 55–69

For women:
1. Cleopatra, II. v. 107–19 (cut Charmian's line)
2. Cleopatra, IV. xv. 76–91
3. Cleopatra, V. ii. 49–62
4. Cleopatra, V. ii. 76–94 (cut Dolabella's lines)

Each speech is about the same length. In the two cases where a minor character briefly interrupts the monologue, I cut that character's lines.

The men's voices are markedly different—the bluff soldier Enobarbus marveling in spite of himself at Cleopatra's splendor; the usually cold, stoic Caesar paying tribute to Antony's courage and leadership; Antony preparing to leave Egypt; and Antony preparing to die. Although all the women's speeches are Cleopatra's, they, too, are distinctive: they show the protean queen in every mood, from jealousy of Antony's new wife to despair over the death of her man of men.

Ben picked the passage where Antony, having been told that Cleopatra has committed suicide, wishes to die. He asks his junior officer, Eros, to carry out his promise of killing him (IV. xiv. 55–69):

> *Since Cleopatra died*
> *I have lived in such dishonour that the gods*
> *Detest my baseness. I, that with my sword*
> *Quartered the world and o'er green Neptune's back*
> *With ships made cities, condemn myself to lack*
> *The courage of a woman—less noble mind*
> *Than she which by her death our Caesar tells*
> *"I am conqueror of myself." Thou art sworn, Eros,*
> *That, when the exigent should come, which now*
> *Is come indeed, when I should see behind me*
> *Th' inevitable prosecution of*
> *Disgrace and horror, that on my command*
> *Thou wouldst kill me. Do't; the time is come.*
> *Thou strik'st not me; 'tis Caesar thou defeat'st.*
> *Put colour in thy cheek.*

We had discussed the context of this speech when we studied the play: Antony is at the lowest point of his fortunes, tormented by remorse at having caused the "death" of Cleopatra (actually, a ruse of hers designed to win his sympathy) and in despair at her loss. Ben pulls a desk center-stage. He takes a seat, looks down, props his head on one arm, and speaks in a low, melancholy tone. Afterwards, the class comments that Antony's despair has come through well but not his strength—his anger at himself and his determination to drive Eros to kill him. "But I thought Antony *was* depressed," Ben objects.

"He *is*," Bill says, "but not *just* depressed. He's really mad at himself—so mad that he's sentenced himself to death."

"Yeah," Meg adds. "He's a great soldier, and he thinks that he was taking out all his sense of failure on Cleopatra. He blamed her for his defeat by Caesar, and now she's dead and it's his fault."

Me: "Do you see that in the speech, Ben?"

"I guess so. I mean, when he says, 'I condemn myself to lack the courage of a woman', I think he's saying, 'I'm so weak and dishonorable that I deserve to die'. He's condemning himself to death. But then why doesn't he kill himself? Why drag Eros into it?"

"What do you think?"

"Well, maybe he's afraid. Or maybe he thinks it's more honorable somehow if Eros does it?"

"What do you think Eros is like?"

"He's young, and he's very loyal to Antony. So loyal he'd rather kill himself than Antony, it turns out."

"Would it help to have Eros there? Antony is talking to him, at least at the end."

"Yeah, maybe it would."

"Okay, choose him."

Ben, who looks more scholarly than soldierly, chooses Eric, blond and boyish-looking, to play his junior officer.

"Before you start, is there a break in the speech—a shift in Antony's mood?"

"Um, yeah. First he's reminiscing about the old days when he was powerful, and then he's complimenting Cleopatra."

"Complimenting her?" Mark objects. "She's dead!"

"I mean honoring her for standing up to Caesar—killing herself rather than letting him put her on display in Rome. I think he even envies her: He calls himself a 'less noble mind/ Than she which by her death our Caesar tells/ 'I am conqueror of myself.'"

"So where's the shift?"

"Well, at first I think he's really talking to himself. Then he starts talking to Eros."

"Why?"

"To remind Eros of his promise. He's got to talk Eros into killing him."

"Where does that section begin?"

"Uh…" Ben runs over the speech in his mind, mouthing the words. "Right after the Cleopatra part: 'Thou art sworn, Eros'…"

"You've got an Eros now. What do you want to do?"

"Maybe I should stand up and face him. Really try to convince him."

"Okay. Are there any other shifts?"

"Yeah—when I say, 'Do't, the time is come'."

"Why?"

"Well, Eros doesn't want to. I mean, right after that he kills himself rather than hurt Antony. Antony must know it's really hard for Eros."

"Okay, let's try it again."

This time Ben begins by sitting and gazing not down but up and out—addressing the gods, in despair but still proud of his former glory. At "Thou art sworn," he stands and faces Eric and appeals directly to him. The pleading comes through in his voice. But watching Eric's face distracts Ben and he forgets his lines.

"Darn! I knew this!" he says, blushing.

"Don't worry about the lines. Forgetting them means you're into the feelings, and those are getting through to us. Let's hear it once more. Pick someone to prompt you. And this time when you get to 'Do it, Eros,' put a hand on his shoulder. He's younger than you are and he's scared. You're the commanding officer, the father-figure."

"Okay."

This time the despair, the self-directed anger, and the desperate last attempt to restore honor all come through. The class's applause is vigorous and sincere. Ben lets out a sigh of relief and, grinning, returns to his seat on the circle.

Mei-Ling chooses the monologue in which Cleopatra is eulogizing the recently dead Antony to Caesar's messenger Dolabella (V. ii. 76–94, with Dolabella's lines cut):

I dreamt there was an Emperor Antony.
O, such another sleep, that I might see
But such another man!

His face was as the heav'ns, and therein stuck
A sun and moon, which kept their course and lighted
The little O, th' earth.

His legs bestrid the ocean: his reared arm
Crested the world: his voice was propertied
As all the tuned spheres, and that to friends;
But when he meant to quail and shake the orb,
He was as rattling thunder. For his bounty,
There was no winter in't: an autumn 'twas
That grew the more by reaping. His delights
Were dolphin-like: they showed his back above
The element they lived in. In his livery
Walked crowns and crownets: realms and islands were
As plates dropped from his pocket.

Think you there was or might be such a man
As this I dreamt of?

I ask Mei if she wants to cast someone as Dolabella.

"Yes. I mean, he *is* there listening and talking back to her—even though we cut those words."

She chooses Phillip, mild-tempered and tall, to play the Roman. She places him at her right and, using a desk as her throne, sits down. Looking up, she addresses the speech to Dolabella, keeping her voice soft and her body still.

"How did that feel to you?"

"I'm not sure I was into it. It felt kind of neutral—like I was talking in a monotone."

"Did it help to have Dolabella there?"

"Well, I don't think I'd really be talking to him. It's more like a daydream, and he just happens to be there."

"Do you ever talk to him?"

"Yeah. At the beginning, that felt right—and definitely at the end."

"Why?"

"He hadn't seen Antony with her and she wants to know if all that was just a dream—like if she's just making Antony up."

"Is she?"

"She comes up with some pretty fantastic stuff—'His face was as the heav'ns', 'His legs bestrid the ocean'. I mean, we're talking God here."

From Eric: "I think Cleo's really lost it. Anyone who can believe this stuff has really gone off the deep end."

Mei-Ling: "But it's not like she believes it. She knows she's exaggerating. What's that word? Yeah, hyperbole. She knows she's talking in hyperboles. She keeps saying it's a dream."

"How does Dolabella feel?"

"He's pretty impressed. I mean, after this he admits that she's right about Caesar—he *will* put her on display in Rome. He's betraying his leader."

"How does that affect your speech?"

"I have to be really convincing. Dolabella is this tough soldier, and he's supposed to be Caesar's man."

"Is anyone else listening?"

"Uh…Iras and Charmian, I guess."

"Do you want to cast them?"

"Yeah, I think that would be good. They were there, they knew Antony. She'd need their support."

"All right, let's try that."

Mei looks around and chooses two of her best friends, Didi and Allison. "Allison, you're Iras. Could you stand—no—sit—on my left? Yeah, right here at my feet. And Didi, you're Charmian. You're standing on my right—and fanning me."

Giggles from the class, raised eyebrows from Didi.

Phillip goes back to his place, then moves so that he is not blocking our view of Allison. Mei-Ling takes her seat. This time, on her first line, "I dreamt there was an Emperor Antony," she puts the stress on "Emperor." That was the title, she explains afterwards, that Antony never got to achieve. Cleopatra wants to give it to him posthumously. She addresses that line to Dolabella. After that, her gaze turns straight ahead, and as she paints the word picture of his hyperbolic powers, her voice gets hushed and wonder-filled. At "his reared arm / Crested the world," she stretches out her own arm. The awe, the worship in her tribute come through.

Afterwards I ask Mei-Ling, "Is anything missing?"

"I think I need to be more sad. I mean, he was a man, too, not the eighth wonder of the world."

"Where do you sense that feeling?"

"In the part about his 'bounty'. Antony was always a generous guy."

"How about saying that line to Iras? She was there, remember."

"Yeah. I'll look at her then."

This time, "For his bounty, / There was no winter in't" comes through with real poignance. The return to hyperbole and the far-off glance, accompanied this time by a smile at the comparison of Antony to a dolphin (a shared joke), are more moving. *This* Cleopatra knows that she is exaggerating, but also that this man was unique and that she will never see his like again. By the time she turns to Dolabella with her last question—"Think you there was or might be such a man / As this I dreamt of?"—her tone has become wistful and child-like—the girl asking if Santa Claus exists. The applause is long and enthusiastic.

Not all the presentations showed this much progress. But those that succeeded had some common factors: a willingness to experiment, a sense of which words were key, an ear for shifts in tone, a readiness to use other actors—live props—to bring out feelings. Most important, the speaker had to be willing to let go—to become rather than to act the character, even if that meant forgetting lines or risking a ludicrous choice to try to reach the underlying feeling.

My role is to encourage the actor to use what he brings to the scene, including so-called faults. Nervous tension can be converted to energy, a block at a particular line can be a hint that the actor does not understand the words. In an essay on preparing for the stage version of *Henry V*, Kenneth Branagh explains the invaluable lesson he learned from his Royal Shakespeare Company voice coaches about "the inextricable bond between textual understanding and technical accuracy." He adds,

> *... if I was continually running out of breath at the end of a particular line, it was more to do with not having the character's thought and intention clear than insufficient intake of breath. If I could find out* why *I was saying something, then they could help me with* how *I should serve it vocally.*
>
> Players of Shakespeare 2, p.101

If the actor is pacing up and down, or "sawing the air too much" in a repeated gesture, it may be an effort to generate energy. Stopping him, slowing the pace, making him savor the pauses, may be enough to redirect that random effort into delivering the lines. For the audience, witnessing this process can be tedious or embarrassing, but it can also be exhilarating. As with any art, the surest means to appreciation are watching amateurs learn it and attempting it ourselves. The goal is not mastery, but experience—not the final performance, but the valuable rehearsal.

Chapter 7

Acting the Short Episode:
Othello and *The Taming of the Shrew*

A more demanding exercise than the monologue is a short dialogue among two or three actors. I used to tell myself that such a technique was the province of the drama department, beyond me and my students because it takes years of training to act or to direct. That rationalization is both true and false. As in any art, training and experience are crucial for perfecting the form. But the essential creative spark, the ability to get immersed in imaginative play, is present in nearly everyone. Acting, like playing a team sport, must be a collaborative effort if it is to succeed. Short scenes do not put an undue burden on the memories and nerves of amateurs, and performing them lets students learn the value of cooperation and of daring. It may also increase their respect for professional actors: There is nothing like practicing an art to make us realize how much work and talent go into making it look effortless. As with the monologue, the aim is not to create a polished, full-scale production but to let students experience the play as play.

Acting in even a brief episode can bring the text to life. It means the difference between passively reading a stage direction like "They fight. Edmund falls" and performing the protracted, painful struggle, complete with groans, slashes, and final collapse. One reason that Shakespeare's plays have remained so vivid is that he writes most stage directions into the dialogue. Those include both actions, like the Doctor's observation on the sleepwalking Lady MacBeth, "Look how she rubs her hands," and reactions, like Bernardo's description of Horatio after seeing the Ghost: "You tremble and look pale." A gesture that passes unnoticed on the page may assume symbolic meaning when it is performed. For example, Othello, duped by the villainous Iago into believing that Desdemona has committed adultery, kneels and vows to take "a capable and wide revenge." Iago, saying, "Do not rise yet," kneels too and pledges "loyal" service in the "bloody business." We are meant to see both the satanic tempter and his credulous victim kneel side by side. The action suggests the devil's role of turning "virtue into pitch" and order into chaos. The "soul" to whom Othello *should* be pledging his own, his faithful wife's, is condemned as a "fair devil." This exchange of vows is suddenly revealed as a perverse marriage ceremony. Iago's final pledge in the scene, "I am your own forever," should ring with chilling irony.

Choosing the Scenes

My first job is to find enough two-character episodes for everyone in the class to act. The selection of scenes depends on the makeup of the class—of males and females, of expressive vs. shy people. Everyone gets a speaking part. Students tend to do best with scenes that focus on brief, pointed exchanges that suggest definite relationships between the characters, and that give each actor some chance to shine. I avoid scenes that contain long passages of exposition or lofty poetry or that are too heavily weighted toward one of the characters. I also try to avoid scenes involving deeply intimate contact. For example, most students find it easier to do the balcony scene in *Romeo and Juliet*, where the lovers are separated, than the first meeting at the Capulets' ball, where they must share a sonnet and kiss twice. The repartee between Juliet and Paris at Friar Laurence's cell and the Nurse's protracted report of Romeo's message to the impatient Juliet also play well. In *King Lear*, the duel between Edgar and Oswald over Gloucester or the quarrel between Goneril and Albany are more accessible than the storm scenes on the heath, which are heavily centered on the mad Lear.

The samples that follow are from *Othello* and *The Taming of the Shrew*. Each list is designed for classes of fourteen to sixteen students. For larger groups, each scene may be assigned to two different pairs. I cast the roles simply by handing out a copy of the list of scenes, with each student's name written next to the character's. The line and page numbers refer to the Pelican editions.

Scenes from *Othello*

1. III. iii. 63–113 (pp. 66–68). Cut Montano's line (82); give Iago line 111 (headed "All").
   Cassio:
   Iago:

2. III. iii. 290–333 (pp. 91–93).
   Emilia:
   Iago:

3. III. iv. 33–98 (to "Zounds!": pp. 100–03). Cut lines 70–77, from "A sybil..." to "Most veritable."
   Othello:
   Desdemona:

4. IV. i. 167–208 (to "Excellent good!" pp. 113–15).
   Iago:
   Othello:

5. IV. i. 212–259 (from Lodovico's "God save you, worthy General!" to his "Whom passion could not shake?" Cut Iago's lines; give "Welcome to Cyprus," l. 216, to Desdemona: pp. 115–17).
   Othello:
   Desdemona:
   Lodovico:

6. IV. ii. 95–168 (pp. 122–25).
   Emilia:
   Desdemona:
   Iago:

7. IV. iii. 10–78 (pp. 128–31).
   Emilia:
   Desdemona:

Scenes from *The Taming of the Shrew*

1. II. i. 1–37 (pp. 61–62).
   Bianca:
   Kate:
   Baptista:

2. II. i. 181–225 (pp. 68–70). Cut lines 209–10; 224.
   Kate:
   Petruchio:

3. II. i. 231–82 (pp. 70–73). Cut lines 249–53.
   Kate:
   Petruchio:

4. III. i. 15–90 (pp. 79–81). Cut from line 49 through half of 54; lines 64–68; and Messenger's role.
   Bianca:
   Hortensio:
   Lucentio:

5. IV. iii. 61–113. Cut Hortensio's role and these lines of Petruchio: half of line 65 ("Fie...filthy"); 90–92; 98–99; 108–109.
   Kate:
   Petruchio:
   Tailor-Haberdasher: combine roles, and call her Seamstress if the role is played by a girl

6. IV. v. 1–48 (pp. 117–18). Cut Hortensio's role.
   Kate:
   Petruchio:
   Vincentio:

Scenes for two actors work best. But because the number of female roles in Shakespeare is limited and because some students can sustain only a small part, I usually have to include some three-actor scenes. Three, though, is my limit. One way of keeping to that number is to cut a role that is not crucial to the exchange—for example, Hortensio as commentator on Kate and Petruchio's spats in episodes 5 and 6 of *Shrew*. If the lines of the minor character *are* important, I give them to one of the principals—e.g., in the first passage from *Othello*, Iago speaks the line designated for "All" in the text. When a scene does require a third character, I try to see that she or he has a substantial number of lines or, if the character is a silent "reactor," I make sure that student has a speaking role in another scene. (In the *Shrew* scenes, for example, the same student played both old men—the vocal Baptista in episode 1 and the silent Vincentio in episode 6.)

I also cut some lines, either because they would be incomprehensible to a modern audience or would make for too long a speech by a single actor. (For both reasons, I reduced Othello's long, poetic description of the handkerchief's magical origins in episode 3.) Since Shakespeare was writing for an audience of listeners, not readers, he often repeats essential ideas outright or suggests them in another line. If not, the actor may usually imply them through actions. Some of Petruchio's insults to the Tailor, for example, depend on a knowledge of Elizabethan clothing and customs. There is no need to keep those obscure lines: Petruchio's scorn comes through at other points. In rare cases, you may choose to replace an obsolete word with a synonym. For example, when Horatio explains how he recognized the face of Hamlet's father, even though the Ghost was wearing full armor, his line is: "He wore his beaver up." Some modern productions have substituted "visor" for the antiquated "beaver." Any teacher reluctant to alter the Word of the Bard should keep in mind that no director, professional or amateur, does a Shakespearean play uncut.

Casting the Roles

I used to think that casting should be democratic, that it had to begin with students volunteering for particular roles. The problem with that approach is that people can be unrealistic about their suitability. Some, overconfident, will want to play every starring role—the Bottom Syndrome, which Shakespeare himself mocked in *A Midsummer Night's Dream*. Others, talented but timid or lazy, will opt for the smallest parts. Having me choose creates a more balanced distribution of parts.

I usually choose students who look the part. But sometimes it works to cast against type—the short, feisty boy for Petruchio instead of the tall, dominating sort; the butter-wouldn't-melt-in-my-mouth girl for the flirtatious Bianca instead of the class rebel. Given the shortage of Shakespearean roles for women, a girl may have to take a male role. When that happens, I pick an episode in which gender is not a crucial factor. For example, the scene in which Petruchio berates the Tailor can accommodate a girl (renamed "the Seamstress") in the Tailor's role. In the scenes where Iago is taunting Othello, the villain may be played convincingly by a self-possessed girl. But both couples, Petruchio and Katherine and Othello and Desdemona, must be cast according to their actual gender if the dramatic illusion is to be sustained.

The Rehearsal Process

How full a production should we do? That depends on how much time is available. At a minimum, I have students do a dramatic reading—a walk-through reading the lines, books in hand. At a maximum, we do an off-book production complete with props and costumes. In either case, the actors begin the rehearsal process by reading the lines with their scene partners. I move from group to group, listening in and answering questions about pronunciation and vocabulary. For example, *zounds*, a shortened form of the oath "God's wounds," should be pronounced "zoonds," not "zownds." *Iago*, Spanish for *James*, has three syllables, "Ee-AH-go," with the accent on the second. *Several* in Shakespeare's day meant "separate," and *presently* meant "immediately."

Sometimes the problem is not with individual words but with the meaning of a phrase or the rhythm of a line. Reading the words aloud at a different pace may be enough, or it may take some phrase-by-phrase translation. I usually start by turning the question back to the actors. If they cannot resolve it, we work it out together, using the footnotes if we need them. Because the actors have to be able to say these words, they usually have a greater investment in understanding them than if they were just reading the scene. Suddenly there is a practical reason for that understanding: to be able to communicate with other people, on stage and in the audience.

The next step is for the actors to get on their feet and try to discover where the characters are going, literally and figuratively. Is the scene taking place in a bedchamber, in the throne room, or on the open road? Is one character sitting down or circling the other or seizing his arm? Is one character trying to dominate or evade or dupe the other? Who has the advantage? I like to pass on to my students a concept that I learned at the Shakespeare & Company institute: Every human encounter involves a struggle to determine who has the power—the will to influence or control the other person. A play consists of a series of such jousts. It is up to the actors to show the signs of dominance, submission, and resolution.

Students are usually adept at using vocal and facial expression. But, left on their own, they tend to do the scenes as talking heads. An actor's tools include gesture and movement; the body should be as expressive as the voice. I devote the first two days of rehearsal to walking through and reading lines, while I move from group to group and direct. If possible, we do this exercise in a large open space like the auditorium or the gym, with groups rehearsing in different parts of the room. If no big space is available, we use empty classrooms. The important thing is for students to feel free to move around and to raise their voices.

What is my role as director? There is no pat answer: I have discovered that directors, professional and amateur, range from autocrats to facilitators, their styles from authoritarian to self-effacing. The former work out the look and pace of every moment on stage and impose that vision on the actors; the latter ask each actor to help shape the production. I am somewhere in the middle; I prefer a collaborative style, with the initial interpretation coming from the actors, the final version shaped by my reactions to their presentation. I think of myself as an audience of one: As I watch the rehearsal, what is getting communicated to me, intentionally or inadvertently? Is the actor playing Iago so deadpan that his sarcasm is not coming through? So nervous that he does not seem dominant? Is Petruchio speaking so tentatively that Kate could easily brush him aside? Is an actor turning his back to the audience or blocking my view of another actor? Is the actor giving an aside addressing it to the audience? Is there a motive that needs a physical equivalent? For example, is a character who is refusing to listen to another simply standing there, or is she turning her back or sidling away? Is the "old" father walking hesitantly, legs apart and back stooped, or is the young actor playing him bounding on stage with a long-legged stride? Is the character being addressed showing some reaction? Is the silent witness to an exchange sitting passive and blank-faced or using expression and gesture to show what she is feeling? Can we add variety to the scene by having one actor sit or lie down or by using a mirror or a flower as a prop?

As with the monologue, I have discovered that it is vital to use any "accidental" feelings or traits that come out. I remember one student, jittery with stage nerves, who was playing Othello. The scene was the one between the Moor, Desdemona, and the ambassador from Venice, which takes place after Iago's "poison" has begun to destroy Othello's faith in his bride. The ambassador is the outside witness who is shocked to discover the terrible change in the once-noble general. Sam, who was playing Othello, kept forgetting his lines. When he started to apologize, I called out, "No, Sam! Use your nervousness." Othello's last line before he stalks offstage is the Iagoan curse, "Goats and monkeys!" Pacing, wild-eyed, shaking, he delivered it with thrilling hysteria—no longer the nervous young actor but the Moor unhinged by jealousy.

A different kind of happy accident occurred during the scene from *The Taming of the Shrew* in which Petruchio first meets Kate. The student playing Kate had long pre-Raphaelite curls. Her Petruchio happened to touch them lightly as he was praising her beauty. She hesitated a moment, and then shook her hair out of his grasp. The pair of gestures struck all of us as a means of signaling his attraction to her and both her annoyance and her unwilling gratification at his interest. The Kate of this scene liked that silent praise, but she was not ready to be subject to the man who could give it. The physical trait had become a natural prop.

Sometimes the physical prop is the actor's size: Simply bringing two characters closer together so that one can loom over or stare up at the other is enough to suggest their relationship. In other words, the blocking emerges from such discoveries, and it is different for each set of performers. A favorite question at Shakespeare & Company is "Who walks on stage?" The answer is neither the character on the page (an abstraction) nor the actor (a real human being) but a combination of the two (the actor bringing the character to life).

Sometimes the performance stops there, with a dramatic reading. Sometimes I do a dramatic reading early in the term with one play and a full-scale performance later on with another. When we are doing more than a reading, the next stage is for students to memorize their parts. Many will find by this point that they *want* to know the part because holding and glancing down at the book is such a hindrance to making eye contact and gesturing. In the course of memorizing, the students may make a discouraging discovery: They know their lines at home but, during rehearsal, they get some wrong or even go completely blank (what actors call "going up on their lines"). Yet if they concentrate too hard on getting the text letter-perfect, they may lose the inflections and the movements that give the words life. They may even unwittingly add distracting motions, such as pacing or arm-pumping, in an unconscious effort to "force" the right words out.

The Shakespeare & Company workshop taught me a method of aiding the memorization process: to have students rehearse in teams—two-actor scenes with another two, three-actor scenes with another three. The actors who are not performing become the prompters of those who are, in a one-on-one arrangement. Each prompter follows her or his actor, out of the way of movements and gestures but close enough to be heard. An actor who blanks says "Line!" and the prompter reads that line in a neutral voice. The actor delivers it with expression. There are several advantages to this "human Walkman" technique. It breaks the actor's dependency on the book and allows her to keep seeing and reacting to her scene partner. It makes the actor *hear* the lines that he has seen on the page and so reinforces their memorization through a different sense. Finally, it indicates which lines are giving the actor trouble. If an actor always blanks at the same point, either she does not understand the line or does not feel it. Sometimes just hearing the prompter say the words will clarify their meaning. Sometimes changing the pace or the blocking—linking it to a pause or a gesture—will trigger the actor's memory. In observing rehearsals, part of my job as director is to look for such aids.

After one set of actors has rehearsed, they switch places and become the prompters for the other set. Two to three class periods are usually enough for each set to get in three or four rehearsals and for me to circulate and give direction. My comments may concern a point of pronunciation: "The Elizabethans said 'Sirrah' with the accent on the first syllable—'<u>se</u>-rah.'" I may give directives about blocking: "When you're saying that Desdemona can 'turn' to anyone's demands, take her hand and turn her roughly: in your eyes, she's a loose woman, a prostitute." I may suggest a whole new way of arranging the scene: having Emilia stand behind Desdemona in the Willow Scene, for example, so that she can direct worried reactions to the audience, or increasing the conspiracy between Iago and the audience by having him sit on the edge of the stage to deliver his asides. The examples below, all based on *The Taming of the Shrew*, illustrate how the look of a scene may change in the course of rehearsal.

Three Scenes from *Shrew*

In the fourth scene listed on the assignment sheet (III. i. 15–90), Bianca is flirting alternately with her two "tutors" (really suitors in disguise). One group of actors began by sitting on three separate chairs. That arrangement created too much distance. Next they tried seating Bianca behind them and having the Latin and music masters share a bench. At that point I arrived to observe. I noticed that the greater proximity helped, but that all three were still addressing most of their lines to their audience: Their relationship to each other was not getting communicated. I suggested that they begin by sharing the bench, with Bianca in the middle. Which suitor does she prefer? I asked. "Lucentio," the actress responded, "but she wants to string both of them along."

"Why?"

"She's—I'm—pretty spoiled. I like all this attention."

"That's really important. How can she signal that to the audience?" I asked. Together we came up with a solution.

When Lucentio teaches the "lesson" from Ovid—really a means of confessing his love during the supposed translations, we decided that Bianca needed to react more: to look into his eyes, rest her head on his shoulder. Hortensio, waiting his turn, should not hear this exchange, but he should see enough of it to rouse his suspicions. That meant having him get up from the bench, take a few steps stage left, and address jealous asides to the audience. When it was his turn to sit down, Bianca moved away. In fact, she used the bench prop to scoot once for each step in the musical scale he pretended to be teaching her. Later, as he was giving his final aside about his suspicion that she preferred his rival, Bianca strolled behind, holding Lucentio's arm. Hortensio turned and nodded: Suspicion became confirmation. We also had the idea of using a prop to show Bianca's preference: She would first appear with a flower in her hair which, during the stroll, Lucentio would have pinned to his cape. Some of these directives came from me, some from the actors; others, which looked awkward or slowed the pace too much, we discarded. Rehearsal should be a fluid, creative process.

Another example of a scene in which the "good" sister gives hints of her spoiled side is the episode where Bianca comes in with her hands tied and is subjected to a rigorous interrogation by the outraged Kate (II. i. 1–37). Bianca keeps pretending to take Kate's side, but in fact is taunting her sister about everything from being her "elder" to lacking suitors. Kate reacts by shouting and striking out, and Bianca's cries bring her doting father to the rescue. Once, after a rather monotonous run-through—all threats from Kate and protests from Bianca—we decided that Kate should be as much victim as aggressor. We changed the blocking to suggest Bianca's provocative role. For example, when Kate struck Bianca, Bianca raised her arm so that Kate hit her own hand hard on the bony forearm. We placed Kate so that her face showed pain and surprise to the audience; at the same moment, Bianca, in profile, saw her old father entering from the opposite side. She shot the audience a sly glance and then burst into a loud fit of weeping. Baptista separated the two, took his favorite in his arms, and began to berate Kate. As he was patting Bianca's back, which was to the audience, she turned toward her sister long enough to stick her tongue out. Most of these suggestions came from the girls playing Kate and Bianca, both of whom had sisters they had wrangled with.

To take a final example, we did the "sun-moon" scene between Kate and Petruchio, in which the newlyweds' power struggle is centered on an old man they happen to encounter on the road to Padua (IV. v. 1–48). At first old Vincentio entered from stage left, but we discovered that that blocking choice took too long and called too much attention to his halting walk. Instead, we had him enter from backstage center and stop between the lovers, caught in the middle, literally, of their contention.

Often, adding physical action is enough to bring a scene to life, but most amateur actors have to be encouraged to touch each other, especially at first. As Petruchio alternately praised and berated Vincentio, I directed him to stroke or pinch the old man's cheeks. I told Kate, who is both obeying and mocking Petruchio's orders, to embrace Vincentio, but roughly. Still, the action felt awkward and restrained. We needed to discover what each person would feel in such a situation and then to get those feelings into the scene. The boy playing Petruchio, for example, admitted that he did not understand why Vincentio would be insulted at Petruchio's praise of his eyes and coloring. We started inventing comparable compliments for him: "Oh, Mike, you're the loveliest girl I've ever seen. Your golden locks, your delicate complexion, your dainty walk—a vision of beauty." He laughed and blushed. The next time, he exaggerated his worshipful tone, and Ken, as Vincentio, reacted to Petruchio's "praise" with surprise and indignation. Sarah, as Kate, couldn't resist smirking at Petruchio. The scene clicked.

The Final Product

As students get involved in their roles, they may want to add costumes and props—a cloak and boots for Petruchio, a real or cardboard instrument for Hortensio to strum, a wig for old Vincentio, a mustache for Petruchio, and rouge for Kate and Bianca. These touches can add to the illusion, but they should be kept to a minimum. The performance can work as well if everyone wears neutral modern clothes (like turtlenecks, jeans, and skirts) and mimes the props. The main force should come from the actors' delivery and the movement.

For the performance, I have found that it is vital to have an audience—another class, parents, a school assembly. Students often protest this idea at first, but most make the happy discovery that actors take energy from those watching them. When an audience is made up of other students, I usually remind them beforehand of the difficulties of performing and ask them to be considerate. If they do not know the play, I give them a brief plot summary and introduce the cast. Whether or not a live audience is available, I also try to videotape the presentation, both for immediate gratification and for future study.

The tape usually starts with an announcement: "The New Globe Players present scenes from *The Taming of the Shrew*." The scenes follow in the order in which they occur in the play. Then the players come out in a line, take hands, and bow. In spite of what can—and does—go wrong in performance, the cooperative effort and the excitement nearly always make the class warmer and more cohesive. Nearly everyone is ham enough to relish seeing himself—and his classmates—on camera. In fact, going back to the standard reading-discussion format can seem pretty tame. But students do not go back unchanged. Something has touched their imaginations; they will see and hear the lines in other plays with a livelier understanding.

Chapter 8

The Critical Essay: *Hamlet*

After two or three weeks of taking quizzes and acting key moments, students should be ready for a longer, more demanding final project. One possibility is a test. But the quizzes have already measured their test-taking skills, and, besides, an exam favors agility over depth. Especially for older, more capable students, a better choice is a final paper that asks them to synthesize some of their insights, and perhaps discover new ones.

Many students will know in general what they want to write about. I used to think that my role was to give them a due date and collect the papers. I have learned since that some benevolent intervention can make the writing process more profitable for the students and the paper more interesting for me. To reassure and perhaps to inspire the students, I hand out a list of suggested topics. The choices are not limited to expository subjects. They include the "creative" approaches that I discuss in the chapters that follow: the invented diary, the parody, and the critique. But not every student wants to or should try one of those unconventional techniques. Some, by taste and mindset, are essayists. I want them to see the essay, too, as a creative paper—not a preset mold into which they pour ideas, but a collage. Writing the paper should mean generating the individual parts and discovering a structure for the whole design.

The process begins with the student choosing a topic. Here are some examples for *Hamlet*, organized by category:

On Character

1. Discuss the importance of a particular character (e.g., Gertrude, Claudius, Polonius, Horatio, Ophelia, Laertes, Fortinbras). How would the play be different without him or her?

2. Compare and contrast Hamlet with one of the other young men in the play—Laertes, Horatio, Rosencrantz and Guildenstern, or Fortinbras.

On Theme

3. Describe and evaluate the ideal of kingship that the play presents. Or of fatherhood. Or love.

4. Reread and reconsider Polonius's advice to Laertes. What are the uses and the limitations of his philosophy? What results does it have for him and for his children?

On Style

5. Discuss the meaning of one of the recurring metaphors—e.g., references to gardens and plants, to the theater, or to hunting and trapping. Where do the references occur? How do they contribute to our understanding of the situation and the characters?

On a Quotation from the Play

6. In the last speech of the play, Fortinbras says of Hamlet that "had he been put on" the throne, he would have "proved most royal." *Would* Hamlet have made a good king? What would be his strengths? His weaknesses?

The suggested length is 1,000 to 1,250 words—4 to 5 typed, double-spaced pages. That is short enough not to overwhelm but long enough to require real effort at developing and shaping ideas. Some of my students think that once they have chosen a topic, they can write the paper in one inspired effort, correct errors in spelling and punctuation, and hand it in. But often what they have written is a loose series of impressions, some out of coherent order, some undeveloped, some contradictory, rather than a tightly constructed argument. The problem is that beginning writers, like novices in most enterprises, see the process whole. Not only are they unsure how to break it into steps, but also they do not know that there *are* steps: An essay, a poem, a book, they believe, is something that a professional author simply sits down and turns out. It flows from the pen, or word processor, in perfect form—with a few misspellings, students might concede, but essentially intact and inevitable. With that misconceived ideal before them, they try to turn out publication-quality work in a first draft, and then are discouraged by what they see as its amateurish level. I try to show them that masterpieces, too, grow from preliminary sketches, and that almost any piece of writing can be approached in stages. For critical essays, the most crucial steps are brainstorming, finding a thesis, searching for supporting evidence, and arranging the parts in coherent order. I am going to describe how I use class discussion and individual writing conferences to teach those skills. My goal is not just to help a student produce a stronger paper but also to demystify the whole process of writing an essay.

Brainstorming

The first step is to gather ideas; there will be time enough to order them later. This is the brainstorming session: Once the student has chosen a topic, he writes down all the ideas about it that come to mind, paying no attention to wording or coherence. He may begin with a description of the character, an opinion, a single word like "father" or "revenge." Although he is writing rapidly and free-associating, it helps to put each idea on a separate note card. That technique takes time at this stage, but later it will save not only time but effort. The student will be able to shuffle through these preliminary notes, decide on an approximate order for his ideas, discard points that are irrelevant, spot gaps in his reasoning. The cards should allow for maximum development as well as maximum flexibility: the greatest number of ideas in their most effective order. The first purpose they should serve is to lead to a strong thesis.

Finding a Thesis

A topic, I stress, is not a thesis; it is too neutral. The thesis must express an attitude toward the topic. It must answer the question: What is this paper trying to prove? Before students begin writing the final paper, I ask them to write a draft of the thesis or, for a creative paper, a description of the approach and bring it to the next class. It may consist of only a single sentence, or it may be an entire paragraph. We spend the period discussing as many of them as possible.

Most students respond to the challenge of knowing that their classmates will see their work. I usually begin by asking for a volunteer, either someone who is confident about her thesis or who knows that she needs help with it. I ask her to write her statement on the blackboard and then read it out loud. The rest of the class acts as a committee of editors: What works, what does not? Where in the play will the writer have to go for supporting evidence? I guide and clarify, but let the class do as much of the editing and advising as possible. The writer can ask questions, take notes, try out new ideas that occur to her on the spot. No matter what the student example, I try to keep the tone light and the criticism supportive. At this time, the beginning of the writing process, people need encouragement as well as direction. Both empty praise and cynical dismissal are counterproductive.

Faulty thesis statements tend to fall into one of the following categories.

The Vague Thesis

The first category is a "thesis" so vague that it is really still a topic. In its most naive form, it sounds like this: "I am going to write about Gertrude." The personal pronoun and the broad subject give away the writer's lack of a real idea. But an only-a-topic thesis can also have sophisticated wording: "Gertrude, Hamlet's mother, is an important and interesting character." As a student editor points out, this might be the first sentence in a paper, but it does not state what the writer wants to prove. This thesis lacks what Sheridan Baker in *The Practical Stylist* calls "the argumentative edge."

The writer, proud of his wording, resists the advice at first. Then a classmate asks what would happen to an essay based on such a central idea. The answer quickly becomes clear: It would lack both specificity and direction. "But how should I change it? What should I do?" the writer asks. The class advises him to ask himself some hard questions: How is Gertrude interesting? Why is she important? To the theme of love, to the characterization of Claudius, to the question of Hamlet's sanity? What picture of her does the writer have in mind?

Often, it helps to begin a character study by using the quiz question about the list of descriptive adjectives. Does he see Gertrude as "selfish," "grasping," "blind," or as "well-meaning," "victimized," and "loving"—or a combination of these two conceptions? A thesis about her function in the play can come out of such descriptions. For example:

> *Gertrude is too shallow and self-indulgent to see through Claudius.*

> *Gertrude's infidelity is the source of Hamlet's disillusionment with the world. Had she remained faithful to her first husband, there would be no* Tragedy of Hamlet.

Both of these assertions may be overstated, but they give the student something to argue. In the process of gathering evidence, he may discover that he no longer completely believes the thesis—that he is tempted to argue against himself. I try to reassure the student that such ambivalence can be a source of strength, that he can write such doubts into the paper: "in the beginning...but later on...," or "At first it may seem that...but on closer consideration..." Instead of excluding one feeling or the other, the writer should make clear that Gertrude changes or that he can see more than one interpretation of her actions. The analysis of a character's motives and feelings, and their effects on other characters, will be richer for recognizing such complexities.

The Illogical Thesis

If a student does not admit such conflicting feelings, though, she may create not complexity but confusion. A girl, struggling with the topic of Claudius's role, asked for help with the following thesis:

> *The king in a way is a good guy. His ambitions and actions make him out as a bad guy, but the real person isn't that way. It's hard to really like the king.*

On one level, it is the wording that goes wrong here—slang ("good guy," "make him out") and vagueness ("real person," "really like") blur the ideas. But a more basic problem is the logic of this argument-in-little: The conclusion contradicts the premises. The confusion came about, the student realized, because she had not made up her mind how she felt about Claudius. There was something in his character that she found strong and appealing, but he was clearly a villain. Instead of admitting that paradox, the writer simply put down one impression after the other. The student editors advised her to trust her instincts about people, including Claudius: As with the Gertrude example, rather than deny her feelings about the contradictory sides of the king's nature, she should admit and then clarify them. Here is a later version of her thesis statement:

> *Although Claudius's ambitions make him do evil things, he is in many ways a loving man and a strong king.*

The Too Obvious Thesis

A thesis may, on the other hand, be perfectly logical but so obvious that it need not be proven. A statement like "Polonius loves to talk" or "Many of the other characters betray Hamlet" is more a description than an argument; the "proof" consists of a list of parallel examples. For example, Polonius holds forth to Gertrude and Claudius, to Ophelia and Laertes, and to Hamlet. That proves it: He loves to talk. Other theses in this category include:

> *Ophelia and Laertes are dutiful children.*

> *There are several references to the theater in* Hamlet.

> *Claudius is responsible for the trouble in Denmark.*

As with the merely-a-topic theses, any of these statements could be part of some larger argument. But if they are made the central point, the reader's reaction is likely to be "So what? Anyone can see that." Such a paper is usually as boring to write as to read.

This is not to say that the too-obvious thesis is a total loss. In each case, the writer has a well-focused topic. What he must do next is ask himself the hard questions about causes and effects. In the first example, on Polonius's children: How does the dutifulness of Laertes to his father differ from Ophelia's? What results from their filial loyalty? Why do love and obedience lead to disaster? How is the form that that disaster takes fitting for each character? Where in the play do we go to find the answers? The class advised this writer to look at each of the scenes between Polonius and his children, the scene where he sends his servant Reynaldo to spy on Laertes in Paris, and the scenes of Ophelia's madness and her brother's fatal duel. In the course of writing the paper, the student also included Ophelia's exchanges with Hamlet in the nunnery scene, the report of her drowning, and the scene of her funeral. The paper grew into a compelling study of the costs of blind adherence to a rigid code of behavior.

The Too-Narrow Thesis

Another student asked for help with this thesis:

> *Hamlet does not take advantage of the one chance he has to kill Claudius.*

The class saw immediately that this statement is too obvious. It took them a while longer to realize that the statement is also too narrow: It focuses on one short scene, and it includes neither the motives nor the consequences of Hamlet's failure to act. A strong thesis, I reminded everyone, has to consider causes and effects. Other thesis statements with too narrow a scope:

Ophelia's death is more pitiful because it is only told, not shown.

All of Guildenstern's lines could just as well be spoken by Rosencrantz.

The pirate attack that saves Hamlet is an incredible coincidence.

Papers based on such points turn out to be more notes than essays. A desperate student may try to stretch the one or two pages of solid argument into the required four to five by using wide margins and adding plot summary. A more productive course is to try to discover in the planning stage a broader version of the statement. The first two statements above, for example, grew into the following:

Hamlet's tendency to see several sides of an issue makes him 'lose the name of action' at several crucial points. Ultimately, it costs him the kingship and his life.

Hamlet *is a revenge tragedy, not a love story. From first to last, Ophelia is not a tragic heroine but a pathetic victim.*

The Too-Broad Thesis

The opposite problem is the thesis that tries to cover too much:

Hamlet *is Shakespeare's greatest tragedy.*

No matter what the occasion, Hamlet comments on it eloquently.

The extended metaphors in Hamlet *help create the atmosphere.*

Hamlet is more complex than the people around him.

These statements are hopelessly wide-reaching and vague. Often the writer is someone who has genuinely enjoyed reading the play. She has understood it from scene to scene, but now the task of synthesizing her impressions overwhelms her. She tries to take refuge in grandiose claims or in impressively literary-sounding topics. Having stated her unprovable thesis, however, she has only a dim idea of how to proceed.

The class may advise her to forget about fancy wording and begin with ideas. What about the play really interests her? Hamlet as a speaker? How about asking herself if the prince's eloquence is always an advantage: Can she think of one example where Hamlet's golden tongue serves him well, another where it is a handicap? Or she might apply those examples to the last paper topic, the evaluation of Fortinbras's praise of Hamlet as king. Is it the extended metaphor idea that has piqued her curiosity? If so, she should limit herself to one—e.g., the references to gardens. She should speculate on what the metaphor seems to mean, make a list of scenes where she remembers that it occurs, and then reread the play to test that interpretation.

The Wrap-Up

In a typical class period, we would not be able to cover so many or such varied thesis statements as I've described here. Not every student would want to risk the public exposure, in spite of the rewards: a moment of stardom and a lot of free advice. Still, as the tension relaxes and the advice becomes more practical, more people usually want to volunteer than time permits. We discuss as many as possible. At the end of the period, I collect the statements we have not covered, saying that I will return them the next day with a brief written comment.

At this point, the prewriting stage is far from over, of course. Students whose thesis statements fall into one of the problem categories have a lot of reshaping and rethinking to do. They may be feeling lost or discouraged. Others, overly scrupulous, may be so impressed by someone else's work that they have lost confidence in their own. Sometimes that qualm gets expressed during the class, sometimes in a scribbled note afterwards. Some honorable souls may hesitate to use the editing advice because it is not their own work. One boy even added footnotes to his essay crediting his classmates for their contributions. Even students whose thesis statements are strong may not be sure what their next step should be. I have found that they can be spared some confusion, and perhaps futile effort, by a stitch-in-time conference with me.

The Conference

In order to see every student individually for fifteen to twenty minutes, I usually have to suspend two or even three class meetings, as well as use any available time before, after, and during school. This is a demanding process for me: It takes much more energy to tutor ten individual students than to teach a class of twenty-five. But the effort pays off in closer communication and stronger papers. Face to face, students ask me questions that they would be too self-conscious to bring up in class, and I get a chance to gauge how hard they are working and what they are like. Close up, the timid, the lazy, the witty reveal themselves and get to have a more personal view of me. For a time, I become not their judge but their coach.

In college, the conference is a regular feature of most writing courses. Students who are not scheduled for a particular day are free to do as they like with that time. In high school, where accountability is stricter, I have found several ways to occupy the rest of the class while I confer with a few. I give them outside reading, show them a videotape of the play, or send them to the library to work on their own papers. If someone misses a conference for no good reason, that person does not get a chance to make it up.

I explain that the purpose of the conference will be for me to critique and then discuss with students one or two pages of the rough draft, which they will bring with them. The pages may cover any coherent section of the paper. Most students choose to work on the opening paragraphs, but some gain confidence or inspiration by beginning with a scene or an example in mid-paper. I either read the pages silently or ask the student to read them to me. What do I look for? In a word, patterns—of clarity, of confusion, of future trouble. This is not the time to copy edit, but to ask some big questions: Is the thesis strong? Is the structure coherent? Are there enough supporting details, including quotations? Are the quotations integrated smoothly? Are there serious problems of word choice or mechanics—malapropisms, run-on sentences, shifts in subject? Does the voice sound fresh and sincere? If not, is the writer genuinely interested in his topic? Is there another approach to the play that he might find more engaging?

I tell the student to take notes on anything she finds useful; otherwise, the whole effect might evaporate as soon as she leaves the room. The main object is to treat these rough pages as a representative sample: every comment could apply to the paper as a whole. I often ask students to turn in this draft, as well as the first thesis statement, with the final paper. That gives both of us a chance to see how far the essay has come from the initial conception.

Why not hold this conference later, when the student has finished the rough draft? Because I want to intervene early in the writing process. In fact, the other concern of the conference is the part of the paper yet unwritten: Where will the argument go next? Where in the play should the student look for supporting evidence? Which speeches or scenes must he include? This is the point at which I advocate a prewriting technique so obvious that I sometimes forget to mention it: rereading the play. This advice often comes as a surprise to students. They've already read the play, they reason; they know what happened. Why do all that extra work? The reason is that this time they will see those passages differently, just because they do know what happened. Lines that seem neutral on first encounter will take on ironic undertones in review; actions that seemed incidental can assume grave proportions. For example, the comic nature of Polonius's officiousness takes on a bitterly ironic tone when we know its tragic results. Shakespeare rewards such close reading because the causes and effects of characters' actions are so clear and the language so fitting.

In rereading the play, I tell the students to take notes, both on their reactions to specific lines and to patterns of action or characterization. Later they can integrate these notes on the reading with their first set from the brainstorming session. If they have done the work on note cards, they can winnow, reorder, perhaps expand the stack. Not every student will be willing to do so much preliminary work. But those who do will be free in writing their first draft to concentrate on how to phrase their ideas. They will not have to worry at the same time about generating and organizing them.

I describe these techniques in class and reinforce them during the conference. Some students need help taking efficient notes—in not putting too many ideas on a single note card, for example. Others may request a second conference later, when they are surer of note-taking techniques or have gotten further with the rough draft. My policy is to put in as much work as the student does, within the limits of time and stamina. Some conscientious few may think that they are getting too much help, that they should be doing the whole paper on their own. That attitude ignores the way that professional editing works and, more important, that students are in school to learn how to write. My goal is for them to write something fresh and meaningful about the play—not a masterpiece but a paper that conveys their own best ideas. (I do not include sample papers in this chapter because student essays are familiar to most English teachers.) The possible fruits of this assignment—sitting down confidently to write a legal brief or a letter to the editor, attending the current hit production of *Hamlet*, chuckling over an allusion to "the play's the thing," reciting a soliloquy for a daughter—are years in the future. It does not matter that by then both the student and I will have forgotten the seeds of such mastery.

Chapter 9

The Invented Diary:
Othello, Macbeth, and
The Taming of the Shrew

Another way to approach a Shakespearean play is to invent a diary by one of the characters. The student puts on the mask of a character he finds compelling and perhaps enigmatic, looks out through that character's eyes, and describes the action. The process is a cross between acting and writing criticism: It means entering imaginatively into another consciousness but then recording, rather than performing or explaining, the observations and feelings. This is the student's chance to "stage" episodes that occur offstage and to supply motives and reactions for a character who does not confide everything to the audience. The challenge is to strike a balance between verisimilitude and originality: to echo the character's voice and outlook without staying slavishly close to the original text or deviating from what is convincing. Like the parody (see Chapter 10), the invented diary must both reflect the original and be entertaining in itself. This is not a way around but a way into the play. It resembles an actor's preparation for playing a role: studying the lines for telling nuances, imagining what the character does in private moments—when she is combing her hair or falling asleep—and inventing responses and gestures. It means presenting some combination of the character and oneself.

Focusing the Paper

How does the writer begin? First of all, by choosing the character. That should probably not be someone who is on stage constantly—e.g., Hamlet—or who confides at length to the audience—e.g., Iago. We learn too much about their private thoughts for the diary to provide meaningful additions. A character who knows himself too little is not a good choice either: Malvolio, the priggish steward in *Twelfth Night*, and Kate the Shrew's coy sister Bianca, for example, are too self-satisfied to be introspective. Nor should the voice be too idiosyncratic, like that of the Fool in *King Lear* or Puck in *A Midsummer Night's Dream*. The best choices tend to be minor but well-defined characters: Edmund, Goneril, and Cordelia in *King Lear*; Emilia and Roderigo in *Othello*; Lady Macbeth and Banquo in *Macbeth*; Claudius, Gertrude, and Horatio in *Hamlet*; Kate in *The Taming of the Shrew*. No matter what the writer's choice, the character should be one that he identifies with and is curious about—one that he understands instinctively but wants to know better.

The next step is for the student to pick a moment that catches her imagination, and to try writing an entry. I have found that the student may not be the best judge of whether or not the diary form is working, so it is essential to have a conference early in the writing process. The student either submits ahead of time or brings to the conference a sample page of the rough draft. I read it, marking places where the mask slips or where there seems to be a lapse in clarity or completeness. If the style sounds hopelessly strained or flat, it is kinder to say so at this point. A few students may persist stubbornly in pursuing the assignment, but most will have come to the same conclusion on their own. In this case, I often suggest that instead of a diary, these students write a critical essay on the character. (See sample topics in Chapter 8.) Since they will already have given the character's motives and actions a lot of thought, they will not have wasted their time. In fact, trying a diary entry may help them understand the character in much the same way as performing the role does. Also, the effort of trying to write in someone else's voice may make the return to the familiar essay format a relief.

A student who has made a promising start may need encouragement—some are too self-critical—and direction about what to do next. How can she better capture the character's voice? One way is to read the lines from a key scene out loud, listening for characteristic expressions and speech rhythms. These phrases do not have to come entirely from the character's own lines or even from the play in which he appears. Someone else's words may be equally apt, and some lines occur so frequently that anyone might use them: "Sirrah?" "How now?" "Is it e'en so?" "He'll have none of it." I tell the student to put all of Shakespeare's words in quotations and follow them with line reference numbers in parentheses, as the student would in an essay. Although that form may look odd in a diary context, it teaches students to avoid unintentional plagiarism and lets me check the accuracy of quotations. In reading the diary, I skim over the line numbers: They are a minor but necessary distraction.

Another way of internalizing a character's voice is to listen to a record of a professional performance. An audio recording is preferable to a videotape because the full production may leave too little for the writer to interpret. A third possibility is for the student to make his own tape of the lines, and then play it back. Once the character's voice is speaking to him, the writer should try another entry. Reading *that* out loud, listening for points that sound awkward or flat, is a good way to test whether or not the diary form is working.

Making the Voice Shakespearean

The lines need not—in fact, probably should not—be in blank verse, but they do need to sound convincingly Shakespearean. Sometimes, a word is too modern—*hugged* instead of the Elizabethan *embraced* or *clasped*, *trip* rather than *journey* or *voyage*, *jerk* instead of *knave* or *caitiff*, *scared* instead of *fearful* or *affrighted*. I remind students that Shakespeare does not use contractions like *don't* or *can't*, preferring instead *do not* or *can not*, but he does contract *is it* to *is't* and *in his* to *in's*.

Sometimes it is less the word choice than the syntax that sounds too contemporary:

> *Just then he came to my chamber in a really strange mood.*

> *What a wondrous thought: Perhaps I might get a chance to observe the Duke in his court.*

As with individual words, the solution is to look for Shakespearean synonyms:

> *E'en then he came to my chamber in a mood most strange.*

> *O wondrous thought: Perchance I might observe the Duke at court.*

Another requirement for writing convincingly Shakespearean speech is to get the obsolete verb inflections right: The second person ends in *st* ("Thou dost"), the third in *th* ("He doth"). If an extra syllable is needed for easier pronunciation, the suffix begins with an *e* ("Thou knowest," "He knoweth"). Some verbs, though, had already assumed their modern form in Shakespeare's day—e.g., the line is usually "She speaks," not "She speaketh," and "He goes," not "He goeth." Overusing the old-fashioned inflection creates an artificial tone.

In longer expressions, too, sometimes the student is trying too hard to echo Shakespearean diction and writes a phrase that is strained or clumsy. The most frequent problems are the following.

An awkward inversion:

> *I pressed him what with the letter would he do.* (Correction: *I pressed him to learn what he would do with the letter.*)

> *Snatch the handkerchief he did, and then dismiss me.* (Correction: *He did snatch the handkerchief and then dismiss me.*)

Wordy phrasing:

> *She trembled upon hearing this, and he did take that shiver as if it were a sign of her guilt in some matter yet unknown to him.* (Correction: *She trembled upon hearing this, and he did take that shiver as a sign of guilt in a matter yet unknown.*)

> *'Twas on the surface all in jest, or at least so I do think.* (Correction: *'Twas all in jest, or so I think.*)

A mixed metaphor:

>   *Slowly, like the patient spider, I am drawing my web upon my brother's inheritance.* (Correction: *Slowly, like the patient spider, I am drawing my brother into my web. When he is stuck fast, his lands shall all be mine.*)

>   *I do fear the long strings of gruesome omens.* (Correction: *I do fear the black shadows of murderous omens.*)

Similarly, an instance of rhyme or blank verse may provide lively variation, but the device can sound strained if it is overdone. A tag-end couplet or a burst of metaphor at a heightened moment usually suffices:

>   From Viola: *I would I had my brother's outer guise: 'Twould hide me from this island's prying eyes.*

>   From Iago: *Zounds, I so hate the Moor! The blackest hollows of hell are fairer than he!*

>   From Lady Macbeth: *Armed in courage, with ambition our dagger, we cannot fail.*

>   From Edmund Gloucester: *I must put down my quill, for my candle is burning treacherously low.*

The Content

Once the student has the voice sounding in her ear, the next step is to go through the play, making a list of scenes in which the character appears or is mentioned, and scenes that he or she might conceivably overhear or be affected by. With that outline before the writer, she should decide on the shape of the diary: When and where will it begin? With a scene that takes place before the start of the play—e.g., with Edmund at school or in military training, during the boyhood in which he was "out nine years"; with Kate and Bianca as squabbling girls; with Lady Macbeth losing the "babe" she once "milked" so tenderly? How much ground should the diary cover? If the character dies, is there time for a last brief entry, or would it be more convincing or more dramatic if the action stopped just before the climactic moment? For example, should Edmund write a few last words after he is "borne off," mortally wounded, or should his last entry precede the fatal duel with his brother? Should Kate's last entry be set before the return to her father's house or ten years hence, after the arrival of little Katherina and Petruchiello? In any case, the diary, like the play it is based on, should have a story line, even an implied plot.

The content of the entries also needs variety. Instead of being all narrative or all the same length, they should differ in pattern and focus. The implied purpose for the character's writing a particular entry should determine its tone and length: a string of curses to express outrage, or a list of tender names to suggest romantic longing; an epigram to express a sudden realization; a leisurely description of a person or a place to reflect nostalgia or love; an impassioned outburst to suggest self-discovery or powerful conviction. The focus may be a description of another character—e.g., Goneril's view of the handsome Edmund or of her loathed husband, Edmund's of the two sisters who are rivals for his love, Emilia's of the charismatic but fearsome Othello. Another possibility is to have the character describe himself, after a glance in a mirror. Is the tone complacent or mocking? What color hair does Juliet have? Does Roderigo think himself attractive? How does Kate see herself in comparison with her sister?

But any background information that is needed to understand a scene must be introduced in a way that is convincing. Iago's slighted wife Emilia would not write in her own diary, for example, "I am three and thirty," though she might well say, "Three and thirty is not old age. The glass doth show I am still fair." The disguised Viola could not realistically describe her duel with Sir Andrew as it is happening, though she would be likely to confide her fear and wonder to her journal afterwards. A character who did not witness a scene cannot record it—unless another character describes it to him or she can be pictured as eavesdropping during it. It is possible, for example, that Hamlet tells Horatio of his quarrel with Ophelia or that Cornwall was listening when the Duke of Gloucester warned Edmund not to reveal that he has received a letter from Cordelia's forces. Finally, no character who dies on stage can reflect on that scene, though some who are carried off mortally wounded— Edmund, Roderigo—might well pen a few last words.

How can such necessary information be conveyed without sacrificing verisimilitude— literally, truth-seeming? By the playwright's own means: a letter planned or received, a speech rehearsed in advance, a conversation overheard. A scene that never takes place on stage can contain crucial revelations of character: Viola donning her brother Sebastian's clothes, Edgar revealing his true identity to his dying father, Ophelia gathering the remembrances from Hamlet that her father has ordered her to return, Claudius poisoning his brother. An invented dream can also reveal hopes and fears. Finally, a scene that takes place long before or long after the play can act as a prologue or an epilogue: Goneril and Regan recalling the birth of Cordelia, Gloucester describing the death of his Duchess of Gloucester before or after the birth of his bastard son, King Edgar in old age reflecting on his reign, Kate and Petruchio dealing with a happy brood of daughters and sons.

To create a sense of place, the writer can describe the prison cell or castle or magical island where the diary is being written. He can include a catalogue—of clothes or books or implements of torture. He should certainly appeal to all the senses—to smell and touch and hearing as well as to sight. The time and location of the entries can also help set the mood: "My chamber, midnight"; "The open heath, near Dover"; "Noon, on the road to Padua." Anything goes that can bring the play to life through the medium of the character's consciousness.

Student Samples

Some students find this hybrid form an ideal format for expressing their understanding of the play. One writer imagined Iago's wife Emilia admiring the beauty and goodness of her mistress and puzzling over Iago's motives:

> *This morn Desdemona and I did buy cloth of gold to make her a gown for her lord's pleasure. She doth outshine the very cloth! Then did we talk of Michael Cassio. She is of "so blessed a disposition she holds it a vice in her goodness not to do more than she is requested" (II. iii. 306–07). The Moor's "soul is so enfettered to her love that she may make, unmake, do what she list" (line 328). Now, even now, she is with the Moor moving for Cassio. But I do not understand my Iago. He wished me to plead for Cassio to my lady. Doth he not want the office? I do believe he is not what he was.*

Cleverly, the writer has put Iago's words in Emilia's mouth, both in the attributed and unattributed quotations (e.g., "Now, even now" and "I am not what I am"). The borrowing not only lends authenticity to Emilia's diction, it reflects the malevolent influence that her husband is having on her judgment of people and events. Like Othello, this writer suggests, Emilia "already changes with [Iago's] poison."

Sometimes the fatal change a character undergoes is self-inflicted. In this diary of Lady Macbeth, two entries show the increasing hold that guilt exerts on her conscience:

> *I must have a taper by me at all times, for in the dark, strange apparitions show themselves in murky shadows, and hoarse lamentings whisper in the empty air. Last night I swore I beheld three gnarled faces at my window, with eyes that burned as if with Hell's own fire, chanting, "By the pricking of my thumbs, something wicked this way comes" (IV. i. 44–45). My voice did stick in my throat, and when I closed mine eyes as not to see, from behind my lids the faces smiled back at me. I have no longer appetite for food nor drink; merely to look on wine afflicts me with violent pains, for in the grapes' redness I see Duncan's blood.*

Lady Macbeth was not present when the weird sisters uttered the line quoted, but it is possible that Macbeth heard it and mentioned it to her. Or perhaps they did appear to her, too, murdering *her* sleep with their accusations. In either case, it is a chilling touch. Two entries later, the same themes of remembrance and accusation appear, but the guilt has caused madness, the nightmare has become hallucination:

> *My spirit "sits in a foggy cloud" (III. v. 35), and now am I "cabined, cribbed, confined, bound into saucy doubts and fears" (III. iv. 27–28). "Out, damned spot!" (V. i. 31). A little water cannot clear us of this deed. Black Macbeth? Macbeth the tyrant? 'Tis not so—is't? Where is the Thane of Fife? More water! "By the pricking of my thumbs"—Banquo's in the grave, my lord—"something wicked"—he cannot rise before thee—"this way comes"—'tis impossible. "All the perfumes of Arabia will not sweeten this little hand" (V. i. 44–45). 'Tis a guilty hand. A guilty soul. Fie, my lord, wherefore are you so afeared? "I have done the deed" (II. ii. 17). My thoughts are bespattered with innocent blood. Another spot? All is red. Even the sky blushes at what it spies. Out, out! The icy palms of all my sins*

wrap themselves around my neck and squeeze. 'Tis cold. I must call for stronger fire burning in the hearth—burning in the heart—burning eyes like Hell's own fire—"something wicked" ...

A third example, from the diary of Kate the Shrew, also concentrates on the changes that the character is undergoing, and at the same time suggests a motive for recording such thoughts:

Padua, Baptista's House
Saturday night

Will I or nill I, it seems I must be married tomorrow to that ruffian of a madcap of a coxcomb, Petruchio! I am to have no say in the matter, they are all so pleased to have their riddance of me. And now what will become of Katherina?

Petruchio's House
Sunday

My hand shakes as I write! My worst fears were nothing next to what has passed today! Did I write the man was mad after conversing once with him? I knew not the half. This day is a nightmare, which, an I wake not from it, will drive me madder still than my lunatic husband. I have ensconced myself a few minutes by the prerogative of feminine modesty, yet even now I hear him raging without, and shudder so that I cannot write. O, I will tell all to my diary, and seek the comfort no one in the world can give me.

I have but a moment. I am all bewildered, for he has not let me eat or sleep with his railing, and yet protests he's moved but for my comfort: The meat will not do him, the bed will not do him, and the more I protest, the more he is contrary and choleric. His voice is a clamor in my ear until I know not whether he be near or far—ah, I see his face yet dancing before me, his hair flashes in the sunlight, and how can I express the power of his eyes? So long as I do not look into them I am strong. I will speak my heart lest it break with shame and anger. I will not be muzzled, I'll not be made a fool, a puppet—O, am I not still Katherina, that was Katherina Minola? These are my own arms, my own hands, I write my own words, and I'll keep my mind and my soul's voice.

The diary is already suggesting, in the midst of Katherine's pride and rage, the powerful attraction that Petruchio has for her. By the end of the diary, she has come to admit and take pleasure in that power, and in the healthful effect it has had on her nature. A later entry shows that revelation developing:

I have been like one blind; but now all is grown clear. I thought I could not be happy but under my own rule and command; I did not know my own heart's loneliness, and fumed and fretted, never knowing why. And now I see I am to be made joyful in spite of myself. What a brave new world of peace and love seems to stretch before me! And what injuries I would have done myself in the name of independence!

Yet I wonder at myself, when I think how I spoke after we had supped tonight. Imagine Katherina preaching to her sister of obedience and proper womanly behavior! But come, he wished it, and I believe, by his laughter, he knew very well I was a little jesting with their disbelief.

The real secrets to Petruchio's success, the writer implies, are not dominance and cruelty but love and laughter—pretending to tame her, he wins her with his dazzling display of her own strongest traits.

The best diaries reflect such understanding of motive and response, and express them in a convincing imitation of the character's voice. On the day that I return papers, I choose some of the most effective entries to be read aloud. The writer gets a moment of recognition. The rest of the class gets a chance to relish both Shakespeare's ingenuity and their classmate's.

Chapter 10

The Parody: *King Lear*

Another variation on the standard critical essay is the parody. Like the simulated diary, this paper is meant to help students get over any inhibiting awe they might feel toward Shakespeare and into a sense of the play's rhythms and values. Some, steeped in "Zippy" and "Doonesbury" comic strips and Monty Python movies, may at first see this option as "easy," a way around the paper assignment and the play. A bad parody may be both. But a successful one demands a real sense of Shakespeare's plot, themes, and language. Through exaggeration or understatement or whimsy, the writer must show the original play in a new light, from a different angle. Yet he must also create a work that is entertaining in itself. The better the parody, the more precisely it reflects—and distorts—the original.

The assignment puzzles some of my students at first, either because the concept of "parody" is unfamiliar or because they cannot believe that they are being given license to mock a work that we have been approaching so somberly. The aim usually comes clear when I provide examples, either from movies or TV shows or from past student papers. One favorite technique of parodists is to do a silly variation on a conventional scene. In *Monty Python and the Holy Grail*, for example, the typical scene of the knight doing battle with the mythic beast is made ridiculous when the animal turns out to be a white rabbit—and a viciously aggressive one at that. Another common technique is to transform the setting to modern times: In one student parody of *Romeo and Juliet*, the heroine was a punk rocker who lived in a Manhattan high-rise. When her earnest, prosaic Romeo tried to scale the building to her fire escape, she shouted down the advice that he take the elevator. At the same time that this version alters the Renaissance setting, it also reflects Juliet's dominant role in the courtship. In contrast, by having her dress like a rebel and shout like a fishwife, it implies the decorum and grace of Shakespeare's heroine.

This last point suggests another source of mockery: to change an unstated assumption about a character. Instead of being handsome and polished, Romeo is buck-toothed and gawky; Horatio is not a selfless friend to Hamlet, but a grasping rival whose secret aim is to steal the Danish crown jewels; "sweet" Cordelia, like her lascivious sisters, is having a secret tryst with Edmund. Each of these examples requires the informed reader to compare the parody characterization with the Shakespearean original: Is the parody effective because there is some truth that the exaggeration brings to light—e.g., as in the first example, that Romeo must be a model of physical beauty? Or because it is an outrageous reversal of Shakespeare's conception, as in the case of the loyal Horatio and the pure Cordelia? The laugh of surprise is reserved for the audience that knows the original play well.

Understatement can also be a source of humor. In Mel Brooks's *Young Frankenstein*, for example, Frau Bleucher, the wild-eyed mistress of the late doctor, confesses in a passionate hiss, "Yes—he was...my *boyfriend*!" The irony is in the contrast between her defiant ardor and her colloquial diction—the ludicrous deflation of "boyfriend" in place of "lover," "paramour," or even "man." Overstatement is also a favorite device. In the duel scene in *Monty Python and the Holy Grail*, the knight is not merely attacked but hacked to pieces, all the while uttering imperturbable truisms about serving God and country. The scene ridicules both the violence of medieval combat and the noble principles of the knights who conducted it. Some of the best parodies mock both historical setting and artistic form. For example, the minstrel in the *Holy Grail* has the task of providing horse-hoof sound effects as he follows King Arthur, both on foot and around the countryside. The Pythons are implying that in historical event as in romanticized film version, the chivalric trappings may be shammed. In *Space Balls*, Brooks's parody of the *Star Wars* movies, the sadistic villain Jabba the Hut is transformed into the gluttonous Pizza the Hut. Subject to the warping rays of Brooks's vision, Jabba's voracity and his repellent appearance take a literal—and ludicrous—form.

Shakespeare himself loved parodying his own theater, most notably in the "Pyramus and Thisbe" interlude in *A Midsummer Night's Dream*. The jogtrot verse, the literal-minded groundling audience (here turned players), the incompetent female impersonator, the sketchy set: All mock aspects of actual Elizabethan productions. Other elements of Shakespeare's parody are not just for his age but are for all time: The company's histrionics, vanity, and hope of reward from a rich patron find ready parallels in every theatrical group. Bottom's egotism, Quince's fussy officiousness, and Wall's stolidity mock types every bit as prevalent on today's stages as the Globe's. Shakespeare, trained actor that he was, had a keen eye for the underlying motive and the ludicrous nuance.

But writing a parody involves more than having an inspired idea for the initial situation or thinking up a few funny lines. After an enthusiastic start, some students discover that they do not know how to sustain it. They may also be puzzled about how closely they need to follow the sequence of events and the language of the original play and, if they have decided on a modern setting, about how to account for the Elizabethan English. What constitutes a good parody? It certainly means meeting Shakespeare halfway: not being dismissive or contemptuous of the original play, not using the assignment as a way of reducing or evading Shakespeare. The aim is not to produce easy laughs but to show a great work of art from a new angle. If a parody is not based on an appreciation of the play's methods and meaning, it becomes simplistic or irrelevant.

Clearly, then, this assignment is not for everyone. In a class of fifteen, typically only two or three students complete a parody. There are no rules and no guarantees. As with the diary, before a student commits himself to writing the whole paper, I have found it crucial to have a conference on one or two pages of the rough draft. I read the sample through, putting an *x* on every line that rings false. Sometimes, for example, the student has a good ear for

Shakespeare's language, but she has gotten too far away from the original play. One girl, trying to parody *Hamlet*, was influenced by *West Side Story*. She was writing a soap opera called *The Rumble*, in which Hamlet is the leader of a gang of preppies out to fight the school punks. His adoring confidante is his teacher, "Miss Gertrude." It had several funny moments, but, predictably, it shed little light on *Hamlet*. With other pieces, the problem is that the style is hopelessly strained or flat. I may advise the writer to switch to a standard essay format, but one that covers the same scenes or characters. Then the "research" he did for the parody will not be wasted. Some students resent being told not to do the "fun" assignment, but most will have sensed before the conference that the parody is uninspired and will feel relieved.

If the idiom and the situation do seem to be working, the subject of the conference can be where the paper should go next: how much of the original play to parody, how to resolve the plot. I advise students to focus on some small part of the original—usually one scene—and to reread it, taking notes on actions, motives, and key lines. This approach assures that their version will follow Shakespeare's lead. With a list before them, they are more likely to write a parody that echoes the play. The targets and the means are as various as the young imaginations that confront the plays. The following examples are from my students' parodies of *King Lear*.

Student Samples

A favorite target is Elizabethan vocabulary and syntax, the Shakespearese that modern audiences have to master. Terms of address and insults are in this category: To Lear: "Yes, your beardship." Of the Fool: "Foul codpiece!" Of Goneril: CORNWALL: "What trumpet's that?" LEAR: " 'Tis the strumpet's trumpet." Each of these writers was alluding to an Elizabethan custom—e.g., that men wore beards and codpieces and that the entrance of a noble character was preceded by fanfare. Each also made the style echo Shakespeare's: "your beardship" for "your lordship," "foul" in the sense of both "evil" and "reeking," rhyme as a means of emphasis.

Here is a more sustained example of this mockery of Shakespearean diction, occurring at the beginning of Alex Haseltine's "Tragedy Is Dumb":

Trumpets, bubbles, and drum roll. Enter Kent, Gloucester, and Bastard (Edmund? Edgar? Edward? Oedipus?)

KENT: Forsooth! 'Tis Gloucester, whose name I cannot spell.

GLOUCESTER: Ho! What be-eth up with thee? How do thine orbs of fertility be a' hangin'? It appeareth that an event most tedious is in store.

KENT: Aye, the division of our sovereign liege's crown. Not a more tedious happening have we seen since young Cordelia's Bat-Mitzvah. Although there shall be many a scrumptious bagel to be had. Would this be thy little bastard Ed…Ed…Zounds, what is his name again?

GLOUCESTER: Edgar, sir.

EDMUND: Edmund.

GLOUCESTER: And a little bastard is he! A scum-sucking, superserviceable, snaggle-toothed, whoreson inhaler of flatulence. A mongrel, snot-nosed, toe-picking eater of roadkill.

EDMUND: Dad...

Both stage directions and other characters confuse the name of the villain, Edmund, with that of his virtuous brother, Edgar. The similarity of their names, possibly Shakespeare's way of suggesting that Edmund is enough Edgar's brother in spirit to justify his final repentance, often puzzles students. Alex has taken this confusion a step further, into the realm of Greek drama ("Oedipus") and absurdity. He also mocks Gloucester's sexual license—he boasts of the "sport" he enjoyed at Edmund's "making"—by giving him a bawdy line more appropriate to the Fool. Finally, Alex suggests the Earl's resentment of the "whoreson" by having him not only call Edmund by his brother's name but also describe him in a Kent-like string of curses. Edmund, playing his Good Boy public role, offers only a mild protest: "Dad..." The characters speak a mixture of modern and Shakespearean diction, the modernisms serving as comic deflation of the formal speech. In the long curse, for example, "superserviceable" and "whoreson" are two of the insulting adjectives Kent applies to Oswald, but "snot-nosed" and "snaggle-toothed" are Alex's own. The rhythms are Kent's—he calls the obsequious steward a "one-trunk-inheriting-slave" and "an eater of broken meats"; Alex's Gloucester calls his bastard son "a whoreson inhaler of flatulence" and a "toe-picking eater of roadkill." Neither set of descriptions is meant to please the squeamish.

The parodist may mock not only Shakespeare's diction but also the lot of the modern actor in attempting to master it, as in Iskandar Bandar's "King Lear, Hold the Mustard":

SERVANT: O my lord, my lord—

LEAR: Control thyself; what is the matter?

SERVANT: Kent, my lord. Kent is the matter. He hath been put in a most shameful state.

LEAR: Shameful state? What speak'st thou of? That Kent hath been...nay, 'tis impossible; no one would commit such a crime against my messenger. Wherefore is he, anyway?

SERVANT: "Wherefore," my lord?

LEAR: Ay, wherefore is my messenger?

SERVANT: Ah. No, thou canst not substitute the word "wherefore" for "where."

LEAR: Come again?

SERVANT: "Wherefore" does not mean "where," my lord.

LEAR: Nay? What then does "wherefore" mean?

SERVANT: "Wherefore" means "why," my lord.

LEAR: "Why"? Ridiculous! Wherefore didst thou learn such nonsense?

SERVANT: Servant school, my lord. And you did just misuse it again.

LEAR: I made no error! Observe: When Juliet asks: "Wherefore art thou Romeo?" she does not mean "Why art thou Romeo?" does she? Why not simply say: "Why art thou Romeo?" and not befuddle everyone?

GLOUCESTER: To follow the meter, my lord.

LEAR: Meter? Do we follow such meter when we speak?

GLOUCESTER: Nay, and 'tis the fault of the producers, who are too cheap to hire decent writers for hard-working actors like ourselves.

LEAR: 'Tis true they are cheap. Enough! As king, I use the holy powers invested in me...
> *Lear stands; religious music is played; choir sings.*
to decree that the word "wherefore" be synonymous with the word "shower curtain," "where" to be synonymous with the word "where."
> *Music ends. Lear sits down.*

Sometimes the parodist puts not only the diction but also the events in a modern context. The humor comes from the parallels and contrasts between the solemn original and the colloquial modern version. In "Il Padrone," Anne Levine set the play in New Jersey and made the old king a Mafioso godfather. As "Cuordelia" listens to him accepting her sisters' flattering speeches, she says in an aside: "Mala fortuna, what am I gonna say?! Just tell it like it is!" The scene continues with Padrone Lear dividing his criminal empire:

PADRONE: Oregano, you get gambling and drugs in Vermont, and hookers in Connecticut, New Hampshire, and Massachusetts.

Awright, now, last but soitenly not least, Cuordelia. Can you top your sisters, so's you can get a third of the property with more stuff than Oregano and Gonero? Go on, shoot.

CUORDELIA: I got nothin' to say.

PADRONE: Nothin'?

CUORDELIA: Nothin'.

PADRONE: You don't say nothin', you don't get nothin'. Try again.

CUORDELIA: I wanna say more, Papa, but I just can't. I did plenty. I done enough.

PADRONE: C'mon, kid! If you don't come up with somethin', you're not gonna get nothin'.

CUORDELIA: I did what I had to do. I can't say no more or no less. My sisters love you so much, what are they doin' with husbands then? When I get married, my husband will get half of my love, but I ain't married yet, am I?

PADRONE: That all you got to say? Do you mean it?

CUORDELIA: Yeah, Papa.

PADRONE: Awright, then, forget it! You ain't no daughter of mine no more!

Anne has made the feelings in the scene parallel those in Shakespeare's play: Cordelia's pride in her own integrity and her determination to be candid in the face of her sisters' hypocrisy, Lear's blindness to his daughters' true motives, wounded pride, and impulsive anger. The insistence on family loyalty, the vast riches at stake, the conflict between the powerful father and competing heirs, and the public nature of the "living will" are all in keeping with both a prehistoric British kingdom and a modern Mafia empire. But since, in the New Jersey version, the prizes are illicit and the language slang, the parallels are rendered humorous.

In "Tragedy Is Dumb," the division of the kingdom scene is supposedly set in Lear's pre-Christian Britain. But it is replete with sly anachronisms and allusions to the theater:

Fanfare, trumpets, and Silly String. Enter Lear, Cordelia, Goneril, Regan, Albany, Cornwall, France, Burgundy, Dopey, Sneezy, and Bashful.

LEAR: Ho! I supposeth it be time for...for...What be the business at hand again?

GONERIL: To divideth up thy crown, my liege.

LEAR: My crown? What for? Not much can be accomplished with a third of a crown. Oh well, dost any one have a sheet-metal cutter?

REGAN: Not the crown on your head, you fool...er, Father.

KENT: I believeth thy blobulous daughter meant thy kingdom, sire.

LEAR: Ahhh. Of course. I knew that, you know; I was just testing you. I'm not senile!

GONERIL and REGAN: No, no, of course not!

LEAR: Well, well, well, well...Do I know you?

KENT: That would be your daughter, sire.

LEAR: I knew that. OK, I believeth I have it this time. I am supposed to divideth up all my land and give it to my daughters. *The crowd applauds.* All right, which one of you doth love us most? You...Um...

GONERIL: Goneril.

LEAR: Just testing. Speak ye first, since thou are the fattest of the bunch.

GONERIL: *Pulls out a script and reads it slowly.* I love you very, very, very much. In fact, I cannot even say how much I love thee. Um...thou art handsome, kind, brilliant, and a snappy dresser. Where did thou get thy shoes? They are so...you.

CORDELIA [aside]: Gaggeth me with a spoon.

LEAR: Thank thee. And you, Nixon?

REGAN: Regan.

LEAR: Ah, yes. How much dost thou love thy papa?

REGAN: Really a whole lot. I am made of that same mettle as my sister.

LEAR: Goneril is made out of metal?

REGAN: 'Twas a figure of speech. But rest assured, I love you just as much as she does.

LEAR: Fantastic! You get the cheese factory as well as all the swamps.

CORDELIA: Oy, vey!

LEAR: And what does my youngest, prettiest, dearest, most beloved child have to say?

CORDELIA: Not a helluva lot.

LEAR: Come again?

CORDELIA: Nothing, zero, zilch, nada.

LEAR: Nothing, zero, zilch, nada will come of nothing, zero, zilch, nada.

CORDELIA: Humph.

LEAR: Why, you brash little strumpet. Your mother, rest her soul, almost died giving birth to you! And me, I've worked so hard for you...I got you that French tutor, I bought you that Mercedes for your Bat-Mitzvah. And you don't even have your license! You barbarous scythian!

As in the first example, the parodist has sensed, and conveyed, the feelings behind the characters' actions: Goneril and Regan's scorn and hypocrisy; Lear's ineptness, vanity, and irrational anger; Cordelia's rebellion against both scheming sisters and foolish father. In both the original and the parodied scene, the old father is losing his grip, the evil daughters are tightening theirs, and the wise child is caught in the middle.

As the above samples show, the most inventive parodies twist not only Shakespeare's diction but also his characterization, either by exaggerating or by reversing elements in the original play. In "Hold the Mustard," Lear tries to discover the form of Kent's humiliating punishment, which in Shakespeare's play is that the malicious Cornwall has ordered the King's messenger to be put in the stocks:

LEAR: Thou sayest Kent be shamed? What enemy would do such a deed? My messenger be placed in the stocks! Unbearable! No matter; the enemy shall lose his head, and Kent will bear shame no longer.

SERVANT: Nay, my lord, the stocks were not the form of degradation.

LEAR: Not in the stocks! Dost thou intend to say some cursed enemy hath imprisoned him with madmen for the night? This explains his tardiness. The evildoer will be hanged and decapitated.

SERVANT: Nay, my lord, sleeping in a room of madmen was not Kent's punishment.

LEAR: Not that either? What was his shame then? Was he tarred and feathered? Were sheep strapped to his forehead? Were geese glued to his feet? The culprit will be mauled, folded, trampled, stapled, mutilated, filleted, burned, hanged, and then decapitated.

SERVANT: Nay, my lord, Kent's complexion is not that of poultry; he wears no crown of farm animals; no honk accompanies his step.

LEAR: What then was his embarrassment?

Enter Kent, dripping with Zesty Italian Dressing.

KENT: "Hail to thee, noble master" (II. iv. 5).

LEAR: 'Tis not what I imagined! Servant, procure some fresh garments. *[Exit servant.]* Kent, who committed this lowly deed—and of what lowly deed art thou the dupe?

KENT: I basted last night in a tub of this unholy Zesty Italian Dressing; wherefore I know not. The perpetrators are familiar to me, however: thy son and daughter.

LEAR: Traitor! Thou liest.

KENT: Nay, I speak the truth.

LEAR: Thou speakst falsely.

KENT: Nay, 'tis the truth. Cross my heart and hope to die, stick Cornwall's boot in Gloucester's eye.

ALL: What?

KENT: Foreshadowing.

ALL: Ah.

The revelation that Lear's true enemy is his own son-in-law is the same in both plays. In "Hold the Mustard," however, Kent's rhymed couplet shows his foreknowledge of how far Cornwall's enmity will go later on. This comic Kent steps further out of his Shakespearean role to become a literary critic for one key word: "Foreshadowing." The audience gets to enjoy both forms of dramatic irony.

In Tom Dupree's Stoppard-inspired "Wheels to Wanton Boys," Lear's supposed senility and Goneril's vanity are the targets. In the parody, Edmund emerges as the master plotter and major character. He enlists Kent as a co-conspirator, defeats his gullible brother, and finally reveals himself as the Fool in disguise. In expanding Edmund's role, Tom not only gives Edmund many of the original Edgar's lines, but borrows—and twists—several lines from *Hamlet.* This section comes just after Edgar has fallen in his duel with the disguised Edmund:

GONERIL: This is practice, Albany. By th' law of war, brother must slay brother, evil deeds must rise, and cruel women pluck out noble men's eyes.

ALBANY: Shut your mouth, dame. Get thee to thy chamber.

GONERIL: I shall paint an inch thick.
    Exit Goneril.

EDGAR: I lie near death. This most certainly is the worst. Nay, it is not the worst. For is it the worst when one may say 'this is truly the worst'? Nay, the worst is when one may not say 'this is the worst.' Thus, since I believe this to be the worst, I shall say naught.

EDMUND: So pitiful! How could Gloucester beget such different issues?

EDGAR: Gloucester is dead, England in disarray. I would I had not lived to see this day.

EDMUND: Brother Edgar. What you have charged me with, that have I done. And more, much more. The time will bring it out. Now, farewell, good brother.

Slays Edgar.

EDGAR: I do forgive thee.

Dies.

EDMUND: This is the excellent foppery of the world.

Enter Gentleman.

GENTLEMAN: Help, help! O, help!

EDMUND: What kind of help?

ALBANY: Speak, man.

GENTLEMAN: 'Tis my lady Goneril. In painting an inch thick, she arrived at a cross-roads. The blue paint did match her eyes, the red her vestments. She could not decide which colour would most become her appearance. Her flawed heart—Alack, too weak the conflict to support—'twixt two extremes of colour, red and blue, burst stylingly.

ALBANY: If there be more, more woeful, hold it in, for I am almost ready to dissolve, hearing of this.

EDMUND: Permit me not to stop you. Dissolve, man!

Albany dissolves. Exit Gentleman.

EDMUND: Many have died in so short a time. The end of the play doth near.

The successful parody not only has to establish a consistent context in which to mock the original but also has to resolve the invented situation. The writers above managed some novel resolutions. Anne simply let the Mafioso plot end where Shakespeare's first scene does, with Goneril's tough-minded response to her sister's advice that they "think" about what to do next: "We gotta do somethin', and soon. Capish?" Iskandar gave the metaphor of Lear's voracious daughters literal form: His Goneril is not only monstrously obese but also cannibalistic. After marinating Kent in Zesty Italian Dressing, she makes "lunch meat" of one of his soldiers. This is the end of Iskandar's "Lear":

LEAR: O anguish, I think I shall go mad! Both my daughters bequeathed my kingdom betray me, and my faithful daughter in La La Land!

Yells and runs off stage. Thunder. Offstage: "You sulphr'ous and thought-executing fires…Singe my white head!" (III. ii. 4–6).

Flash of lightning and more thunder as Lear is struck by a lightning bolt. Sound of falling body.

REGAN: *[Looks toward sky.]* Good shot! Goneril, finish them off.

Goneril advances on Kent, Edgar, Gentleman with outstretched arms and a maniacal smile.

EDGAR: Gods above! What heavenly intervention will protect us now? The king's a charcoal briquette, and his daughter hungrily advancing!

KENT: Quickly! Appetite-suppressant! Godspeed!

Gentleman fetches chest while Kent and Edgar retreat from advancing Goneril.

KENT: The Grapefruit Diet! Perfect!

Kent and Edgar pelt Goneril with grapefruits; those thrown near her she catches and bites off a part of; others on the floor she picks up and messily chews through.

EDGAR: It works! See how she slows! Our charbroiled king shall yet be avenged. Now if only we had some watermelons!

Entire troupe continues offstage. Curtain.

Tom ends "As Wheels to Wanton Boys" with a Stoppardesque flourish:

Enter Cordelia. Kisses Edmund.

CORDELIA: My love.

EDMUND: My queen.

CORDELIA: I have insured that my father will trouble us no longer.

EDMUND: Excellent! Our plan has reached fruition.

KENT: If Fortune brag of three she loved, we are most certainly they.

EDMUND: Edmund, King of England!

CORDELIA: Cordelia, Queen of England!

KENT: Kent, Gentleman of England!

EDMUND: Gods do indeed stand up for bastards!

CORDELIA: Never shall we fall!

KENT: Never, never, never, never, never!

EDMUND: The oldest hath borne most; we that are young Shall never lose so much, and live more long!

Suddenly everyone freezes. A light blue glow illuminates the stage. A booming voice is heard throughout.

BOOMING VOICE: Ho! Good sport! Give the wheel another turn!

The blue glow disappears. Edmund resumes, as if nothing has happened.

EDMUND: Cordelia, our sons shall be strong, our daughters fair. We shall love them with rich, o'erflowing hearts. When I grow old, the sway, revenue, and execution of the rest shall be theirs. This coronet shall I part between them. Which, I wonder, shall love me most...

Curtain.

Tom has given literal form to Edmund's despairing pronouncement: "The wheel is come full circle; I am here" (V. iii. 175). In the parody, he thinks himself triumphant, but he ends by unwittingly assuming his defeated monarch's fate. *Endgame*-like, the absurd tragedy begins all over again in its final moments.

In Alex's play, Lear becomes so disgusted by the grasping nature of his daughters that he declares he will not divide his kingdom. After protesting in vain that then the play cannot go on, Goneril and Regan take drastic measures:

GONERIL: You leave us no other choice. All right, fellas, come on in!

Enter Hamlet, Macbeth, Julius Caesar, Othello, and Titus Andronicus.

LEAR: Who are these boobs?

REGAN: These "boobs" are men who know how to do a tragedy.

GONERIL: You could learn a few things from them.

HAMLET: Ooorken doorken sploorken to be or not to be.

OTHELLO: Yo! W'as up, home boy?

JULIUS CAESAR: Et tu, Fellatio?

MACBETH: Toomorrroo an' toomorrroo an' toomorrroo…

TITUS: Duh…

LEAR: Oh, go away!

REGAN: We're going to have a tragedy anyway.

LEAR: No, you're not!

CORDELIA: We sure are. I can't believe you're making this so difficult. All right, everybody. Let's start.

Massive death scene. Everyone gangs up on Caesar and stabs him. He mumbles something in Latin too obscene to print. Titus decapitates Macbeth, who strangles Othello. Hamlet gets ready for a big speech about the insignificance of belly button lint when he is killed by France, who also kills Albany, who kills Titus. France, dismayed, runs himself through. Gloucester blinds himself and then kills Edmund, who in turn kills Gloucester. Cornwall has a heart attack. Goneril kills Regan, and then kills herself. Cordelia hands Lear a dagger that she then impales herself upon. All attendants run themselves through on their swords. Kent lights himself on fire and runs around laughing until he drops dead. Finally Lear is alone with twenty-odd bodies heaped at his feet. Enter William Shakespeare.

SHAKESPEARE: My, my, my. I've outdone myself this time.

LEAR: Who are you?

SHAKESPEARE: I'm Shakespeare. I wrote this play.

LEAR: Well, you've done a fine job. Everybody's dead! And weren't we talking in Elizabethan English before?

SHAKESPEARE: I got tired. It happens, you know. Well, I just stopped by to tell you that I've written in a cardiac arrest and that you have about forty seconds to make a

powerful speech before you die. See ya.
> *Exit Shakespeare.*

LEAR: Is this the promised end? Forsooth…oh, no, I can't remember any of my lines. But wait…I think I know the answer now. The true meaning of the universe! The reason that everybody puts up with the handfuls of excrement that are flung in our direction each day. The answer is so simple. All one has to do is…
> *Lear dies.*
> *Curtain.*

In this parody, as in the original, the questions about the reasons for human suffering, the meaning of life, are left open: Are there "justicers above" or are we "to the gods as flies to wanton boys," who "kill us for their sport"? This comic Lear, like his tragic original, is cut off in mid-illusion that he has at last found solace and hope. And he is surrounded by the bodies of his fellow tragic heroes, who have killed one another or themselves with comic speed and ruthlessness. In other words, silly as this collage is, it contains some clear parallels to Shakespeare's outlook, and its very outrageousness makes us appreciate his scope.

I keep the means of sharing the parodies simple. The day that papers are due, I separate out the parodies from the critical essays and read the opening line of three of them in a row. Then I ask the class to vote on the one they want to hear. That author casts a dramatic reading, taking a role himself if he wishes. This is not a full-scale production: The actors cluster around the one copy of the script and pass it back and forth among themselves, as in a crude radio drama. The rest of us sit back and enjoy. For the writer, often not the star literary critic in the class, it is a heady experience to hear his classmates' laughter. For the audience, it provides the insider's pleasure of being in on the jokes. We who have studied the play have become privileged listeners. The more fully we have understood *King Lear*, the deeper our appreciation of the parody's comic slant on its style and content. This seemingly irreverent technique is in fact a backhanded form of tribute. It is also a means of overcoming students' awe of the Great Name. Like drawing a mustache on the Mona Lisa, poking fun at Shakespeare can make him seem both more human-size and more great.

Chapter 11

Director's Choices: Branagh's *Henry V*

Students in an English class can't just talk about or perform Shakespeare; they should also learn how to write about the plays. But as every teacher knows, student essays are often not compelling reads. One reason is that many students dismiss their feelings about the play, which in fact form the basis for all criticism worth reading, as trivial or obvious. They envision their audience not as a real person but a generic English Teacher, and assume a voice that is self-conscious and stilted. When, on the other hand, these same students are discussing the play in class, they are often fresh and insightful. If we happen to be watching a videotape, they often tend to be more acute observers than I am. A kind of paper that uses such acumen was first suggested to me by one of my own teachers, Professor Miriam Gilbert, at an NEH summer seminar on Shakespeare's Text and Theater. The assignment is to critique one scene from a videotaped play. This is not a general "I liked this, I didn't like that" account but a critique with a central focus: to describe and evaluate the choices that the director has made.

Here is the procedure: After we have read and discussed a play, I show a tape of the entire production. Then I ask the class to single out three or four scenes that they found especially memorable. I tell them that I will show just those scenes again, so that they can take notes on the choices that the director made in staging them. But first we talk about the kinds of choices that are available. I list them on the blackboard and then include an edited version with the assignment.

Last year, for example, I had just finished reading and discussing *Henry V* with a group of seniors. The play is so grounded in British political history that it is difficult for Americans to appreciate. I had not taught it for several years, preferring as history plays either the action-filled *Henry IV, Part 1* or the poetic *Richard II*. But with Kenneth Branagh's stirring film version just out, I decided to try *Henry V* again. Several students had seen the movie on the full screen, the ideal format for both the battle scenes and the panoramas. The videotape does, nevertheless, give some sense of that scope and also suggest the subtleties of the power struggle in the tête-à-têtes. We watched the tape in two long showings. Then I asked the class to choose a scene and to discuss Branagh's choices in directing it. What kinds of choices? someone asked. In one brainstorming session, we came up with the following categories:

Casting
Costuming
Makeup
Lighting
Set
Color scheme
Camera angles
Blocking
Gestures
Lines omitted
Lines and words emphasized
Vocal tone and inflection
Sound effects
Background music
Props
Place of the scene in the context of the whole production

The exact assignment was:

> *Write a paper (750–1000 words) on the choices that Kenneth Branagh made in directing a scene from* Henry V. *Some factors to consider are: (The list of categories from the blackboard followed.)*
>
> *The big questions are: What do you see and hear? What feelings do those sights and sounds create? How consistent and how effective is the total impression that the scene creates?*
>
> *After you have taken notes on the film version, reread the scene while the visual impression is fresh. Note any contrasts between the way that you saw the scene in your imagination and the way that Branagh presents it. See the tape again if you have time. In writing the paper, be as specific as possible, and remember to include quotations.*

After a bit of discussion, students settled on four scenes that they found especially moving: the entrance of the young king and and his dealing with the "tennis balls" challenge from the Dauphin (I. ii., in particular lines 223–310); the scene in which Henry confronts the traitors among his own company (II. ii); the Saint Crispin's Day call to arms (IV. iii); the aftermath of the Battle of Agincourt (IV. vii. 51–174, and IV. viii., which Branagh cuts and combines). The courtship scene (V. ii. 98–271) was a close fifth, but we had talked about it after the final showing, and most writers wanted to start fresh. Another factor was that most of the class, male and female, wanted to focus on the young king's struggle for power, its course and its personal cost.

Sample Papers

The papers were not perfect. Some got repetitive or went wrong in some of the same ways as other critical essays, as noted below.

A vague thesis:

Branagh's many choices have an effect on the audience.

Branagh's version brings alive a scene which in Shakespeare had little life but lots of potential.

A statement of empty praise:

This is an excellent example of Branagh's smart choices, as both an actor and a director.

Branagh is effective in capturing the emotions, sights, and sounds that Shakespeare wanted to deliver to his own audience.

An inaccurate detail: One writer claimed that the setting in which the traitors were caught resembled "a locker room," and then went on to take that simile literally: "Symbolically, a locker room would be a very likely place for traitors to be exposed and punished. In modern literature, it is a very masculine setting where men compete and bond."

A misread tone: Another student saw the view of war in the film as not only "bleak" but also "cynical," thus ignoring the implication that courage and resourcefulness are commendable in war as in peace. While Branagh is realistic about the human costs of victory, he never makes us lose respect for Henry the soldier or side with the arrogant French.

Still, every paper contained some fresh and striking insight into the film, the play, or both. Several students invented a title that suggested both the scene they had chosen and their attitude toward it: "A Treasure of Tennis Balls," "Another Fall of Man," "A Prayer for the Common Man," "We Band of Brothers."

The critiques themselves were as individualized as the viewers. Here, for example, are excerpts from three papers on the St. Crispin's Day scene. The first describes the scene's context, in the play and in the film:

The scene (IV. iii.) occurs just before what will be the final and decisive battle in the ongoing war between the English and the French. Not only do the French have five times as many troops as the English, but also they are five times as well prepared, for all of their men are "fresh," whereas the English are "all besmirched with rainy marching." In short, things do not bode well for England, and Henry is hardly ignorant of this fact. His only hope for success lies in his faith in God and in his ability to convince everyone else of this faith. In order for Branagh to pull this off, he must make Henry inspire his men, and by doing so, the audience, with such eagerness and trust that both will believe that anything, including victory, is possible.

Another student commented on the effects of the casting:

Branagh casts himself as Henry. This casting is suited to Branagh's portrayal of the character, as a man humble with those that praise him and strong with those that doubt. He is appropriately young to play the role of Henry V, and he even plays up his youth. His face is always clean-shaven, and he is dwarfed by his broad, bearded Uncle Exeter. His physical presence does not command the respect of his subjects and his audience. Therefore, Branagh plays Henry as having inner strength and the ability to encourage. This is shown explicitly in his St. Crispin's Day speech.

She went on to describe Branagh's use of setting:

The scene takes place outside at the virtually barren English army camp. The forest is not dense, and the trees are all leafless. In the background, the sky is pure white. The appearance of a chill is confirmed by the frost that clings to Henry's breath as he speaks. The one manmade object in this setting is a large wagon, made from wood. With this sparse army base, Branagh confirms Henry's reliance on nature and God.

A third writer also described the cold and the light:

The lighting is what one notices first in this scene. Kenneth Branagh films the scene early in the morning, a morning without sun. This lighting conveys more than a quality of light. It shows cold and depression. We see the cold in every character's face, in the red of Henry's cheeks and nose. It is as if even the weather has turned against the king, for this is a morning better spent in bed than on the battlefield.

Other students were especially adept at noting Branagh's departures from Shakespeare's text. Here are two examples, one on the opening scene and one on the episode in which Henry exposes the traitors among his own nobles:

Branagh makes Henry's character obvious as much through his actions as with his words. Thus, he cuts lines that are repetitive, or can be conveyed physically. Most of the lines he leaves out describe Henry's deep religious conviction or repeat the theme of the recklessness of his youth. Henry's religious side is symbolically represented by the two bishops who stand on either side of his throne. The question of Henry's younger days is briefly mentioned, but Branagh places greater emphasis on his present maturity. He also minimizes the verbal threats Henry makes to the French.

Branagh's first major departure from the text of the play is to have the Chorus's introduction directly precede the scene with the traitors. Shakespeare separated these two with the scene involving Nym and Bardolph. Branagh's choice makes sense as the Chorus speaks of Cambridge's, Scroop's, and Grey's treason, and of the campaign against France. Nym and Bardolph are not mentioned. The purpose of a Chorus is to inform readers both of actions that are left out of the play and also what the future holds. Branagh's juxtaposition of these scenes adds to the dramatic irony and builds our respect for Henry's intelligence in dealing with the traitors.
The Chorus speaks from the cliffs of Southampton, a sparse and bleak setting. He begins: "The French, advised by good intelligence/...Shake in their fear" (II. Cho. 12, 14). This emphasizes the English army's strength, but the Chorus's tone matches Henry's—it is not one of overconfidence. When he describes the "three corrupted men" (II. Cho. 22)—Cambridge, Scroop, and Grey—they are paraded before us, as criminals. The background music swells, adding a sense of tension. The men walk near the edge of the cliffs—suggesting none too subtly their future sentence.

All these writers begin by describing what they see and hear, then go on to evaluate the effects of those sights and sounds. It is this combination of fact and interpretation that gives the critiques their authority. I want students to understand that all these readings are valid. I want them to see, too, that no production of a play is definitive or sacrosanct, especially with Shakespeare. His own stage directions are so spare, his ambiguities are so rich, and theatrical conditions and English words have changed so much since his day, that every production is an interpretation. It is a combination of the director's and the actors' reading, like a group critical essay, except that it is staged rather than written down.

A critic can posit more than one reading of a line or a gesture. For example, he may argue that Lear is either surprised or angry or both as he echoes Cordelia's "Nothing?" Lady Macbeth's swoon may either be feigned—an attempt to distract the courtiers from Macbeth's overacting his shock at Duncan's death, or it may be genuine—a foreshadowing of her later breakdown. A director does not have that luxury. Her task is not speculation but action. At countless such moments, she must choose an interpretation of a line and the means to suggest it. She must also make her choices consistent with one another, so that the production becomes a coherent whole.

Viewers, particularly inexperienced viewers, may take such choices as gospel and believe that some directorial innovation is literally in Shakespeare's text. Students who have watched Franco Zeffirelli's *Romeo and Juliet*, for example, may believe that Shakespeare directed Romeo, gymnast-like, to climb the balcony or that a singer at the Capulets' ball distracted the other guests and allowed the lovers to meet. This kind of naive assumption is a good argument for showing a tape *after* studying the play. Students may agree or disagree with the effectiveness of a director's choice, but they should be aware that a choice has been made, and that their own reactions to the play have been influenced by it.

The Group Essay

The day that the critiques are due, I tell students who wrote about the same scene to sit together and exchange papers. I ask everyone to write a brief comment on one positive and one negative feature of the paper they read. Then we talk in general—no names allowed—about what reading someone else's essay has taught them. The day that I return the papers, we do a group essay on one or more of the scenes: I bracket the best observations, anything from a sentence to a full page, put them in order of chronology or emphasis, and ask students to read them aloud. Together, they form a balanced critique of Branagh's key choices. Here, for example, is a series of excerpts from different papers on the opening scene.

An introduction, describing the context of the scene in both Shakespeare's play and in modern film history:

> *In any production, whether a play or a movie, the first scene is of great importance. Since it sets the mood and the tone of the production, the director must pay close attention to how this scene is played and how it affects the performance that follows. In Kenneth*

Branagh's version of Shakespeare's Henry V, *the opening is especially vital to the rest of the movie. As the star of his film, Branagh decided to cast himself: small, friendly, blond, and looking several years younger than he actually is. In order to overcome the obstacle of his appearance, his actions in the first scene had to convince the audience that it was watching a military legend who would soon win the Battle of Agincourt. In this daring attempt, Branagh couples the modern technology available to him with his own choices as a director to create not only the required image but also a unique movie. His use of lighting, music, sound effects, and camera angles nicely complements his own acting and directing decisions. Using everything at his disposal, he is not only believable as King Henry but also exciting and frightening to watch.*

A different introduction, describing the predominant mood:

In Kenneth Branagh's film of Shakespeare's Henry V, *the opening scenes introduce the characters and set the tone of the movie. The viewer's first and lasting impression of Henry and his supporting cast is formed during the scene in the chamber of the palace, when Henry hears from Canterbury about why he should attack France, and then from one of the French ambassadors about the Dauphin's response to Henry's French claims. This scene establishes Henry as a subtle yet commanding king who has transformed his youthful wildness into a respected royal presence. Furthermore, it emphasizes the mistrust, suggested in the play, between the clergy and the royalty. Yet both these impressions are part of the larger atmosphere this scene creates: that of tension and suspicion.*

Another writer's description of this same mood, and comment on the effects of lighting and camera angles in establishing it:

The set is scarcely lit in Branagh's opening shot of Act I, and everything but the faces of the two bishops, Canterbury and Ely, is dark brown, from the walls to their cloaks. The faces are sepia. The flicker of the candle illuminates barely enough to allow the audience to see the bishops' faces—and, at that, only half of each face is well-illumined. Although the camera films the whispering bishops in full face, only the right half of Canterbury's face is illumined; the left is in shadow. The opposite is true of Ely. Not only is the absence of light instrumental in creating the air of subterfuge, but also the camera establishes the existence of conspiracy. The first frame after Canterbury enters silhouettes both bishops face-to-face. Coupled with the business of Canterbury's door locking upon his entrance and the hushed voices with which the bishops speak, this framing secures the impression of the clandestine nature of their intercourse. At this same time, however, the spartan surroundings and monklike attire of the bishops set the tone of sincere religious devotion and dedication to one's job in life. This tone is characteristic of Henry, too, as evidenced in the next scene.

Another writer on the use of camera angles and lighting to characterize Henry himself:

The camera shots contribute to the concept of Henry's power. Instead of seeing him immediately, the viewer is drawn through the aisle as heads bow on either side in a show of respect. The voyage concludes at the pinnacle of power: the throne. The actor who plays Henry does not seem physically imposing by mere sight. His dress is dark, his figure small. Indeed, it is notable that Branagh chose a throne that appears to dwarf the king, though a smaller one might have lost the importance that the mere presence of such a seat gives.

As with the Canterbury/Ely scene, Henry's throne room is dimly lit, though multiple torches burn along the walls. Branagh is careful to set up the lighting properly. By having Henry's throne against a wall, and the rest of the court's seats in front of the torches, he sets up a powerful visual effect. While the others are lit from the back as well as the front, Henry's face is lit mostly from the bottom and diagonally towards the sides. The shadowing effect, combined with the flickering caused by the natural firelight, produces an almost magical suggestion of power and intelligence. Henry's posture, which has him leaning on his right arm, makes him seem relaxed, as if this power comes naturally to him.

Another on the effects of blocking and music:

The way in which Branagh has chosen to have Henry enter the audience hall helps create the impression of greatness. The audience first hears the sound of marching, then sees the shadow of the king walking with two armed guards. The shadow is larger than life. The music starts with a leaping harmony. Next, the audience sees the milling noblemen, who seem to be waiting for the king. The instant the doors open for the king, the noblemen scatter to their respective chairs and stand waiting for him: In effect, they are mice in comparison with him. Again, the audience sees Henry's silhouette, this time filling the great doorway. Henry marches in and sits down, and the noblemen sit with him. They mirror his every move, but the king remains the original copy.

Three descriptions of the contrast between Henry's power and his appearance:

The king's entrance is marked by the double doors swinging open and regal music rising up in the background. Mr. Branagh chooses to play the king's entrance as self-assured and controlled. Henry parades in with a comfortable, measured pace, while white light streams in around his body. Henry's slow echoing pace and his silhouette give an imposing first image of the king. The music and sounds of Henry's echoing step build up the dramatic tension of his entrance.

The entrance of the king causes the milling lords to rush to their respective positions. Each one in turn bows and faces the king. The audience gets its first clear glimpse of the king when he slumps down onto the throne. His boyish appearance is startling in light of the respect that his lords give him. Henry speaks his first line casually, but with a biting undertone, "Where is my gracious Lord of Canterbury?" (I. ii. 1). His casual demeanor lets the audience know that he is comfortable in his exalted position. Yet his biting tone lets his vassals know that, despite his previous reputation, he takes his role seriously.

Branagh has set the scene for Henry's grand entrance. To establish the king's authority, Branagh has chosen to have Henry enter after all of his lords. Henry's entrance is staged so that he appears larger than life. From the start, Branagh gives Henry a commanding presence. As Branagh directs it, Henry's first appearance is both stately and mysterious. Shadows mask his face as the light pours in from behind. Each lord looks upon the king with respect and pride as Henry passes them. By the time he reaches his throne, there is no doubt in the audience that this must be an extremely worthy and highly respectable king.

Branagh then reveals the other side of Henry. In casting himself as Henry, Branagh ran the risk of appearing young and inexperienced. This, however, is not so. Juxtaposed with his grand entrance, his first true appearance leaves him looking like a fair-haired youth, slouching in his throne. Yet his matter-of-fact, easy-going manner quickly gives him control of the situation. Branagh's appearance reminds the audience that this king, though all grown up, was once the wild Prince Hal.

The audience does not see Henry's full face until he sits down in his large but simple wooden chair and turns toward the camera. By holding back his appearance for so long, Branagh creates suspense for his viewers and, in a way, forces the audience to bow to the king as well. When Henry's face eventually appears on the screen, it has a stunning effect. He looks like a boy of thirteen or so, not old enough to be king at all. He wears deep blue eyeliner, and his round cheeks and pinkish complexion make us think twice about his age. Is he really twenty-five? Perhaps Branagh cast himself because he knew that his appearance would pose a shock to an audience and force us to question Henry's strength as a ruler, just as he questions his own ability to wage war. He asks Canterbury to "justly and religiously unfold why the Law Salic, that they have in France, or should or should not bar [England] in [its] claim."

A different writer's comment on the court's reactions:

Shakespeare does not dictate what the actors should be doing as they are speaking. After the entrance of the bishops, Canterbury prattles on for sixty lines about how "no woman shall succeed in Salic land" (I. ii. 33–95). But such a tirade would bore modern audiences. Branagh must show that the bishop is boring the nobles without actually boring us. He uses a simple, yet ingenious, device. When the bishop begins the speech, he is standing by Henry's throne. As he speaks, he slowly walks by the nobles, with the camera following him, until he is at the opposite end of the room. At this moment, he delivers his emphatic point about the "defunction of King Pharamond," and he slaps the papers he is holding in his hand. At the sound of the slap, the camera angle switches to a view down the length of the nobles, and they immediately turn their heads toward the bishop. Obviously they were not paying attention.

Another student on Henry's reaction to Canterbury's plea:

Following the bishop's drawn-out explanation of the reasons to wage war on France, Henry proves his strength and prudence when he asks, "May I with right and conscience make this claim?" (I. ii. 96). As he delivers this line, low string chords emphasize Henry's scrupulous thoughts about the fatality and danger of war. The camera focuses in on Branagh's face so that it fills the screen—we are no longer aware that his body does not fill the throne. Here Branagh augments Shakespeare's subtleties and clearly indicates that Henry will be a strong leader.

Branagh's choices of music and blocking heighten and presage the excitement and triumph to come in the rest of the drama. The original theme from the march which accompanied Henry's entrance returns, producing restless excitement. This mood reflects the Bishop's invigorating words to Henry:

> *Gracious lord,*
> *Stand for your own, unwind your bloody flag,*
> *Look back into your mighty ancestors;*
> *…invoke [their] warlike spirit…*
> $$(11. 100–04)$$

Here the two bishops face Henry so that they are in profile while he looks straight at the camera. This shot creates an impression of Henry's susceptibility to persuasion. Yet he does not look at them as they speak. Branagh suggests that Henry's reasons for waging war on France are not the bishops' contrived reasons but his own thoughts of future power. The duality of Henry's character is evident: While he is advised by the elder bishops, he proves to be an independent, strong leader.

Two other students on the effects of casting and blocking the supporting roles:

Another way Branagh enhances his power as Henry is through casting. In sharp contrast to Branagh is the Duke of Exeter, who is the king's most trusted lord, and who sometimes serves as the "legs" or the physical aspect of the power of the throne. The fact that someone as physically superior as Exeter is completely at the will of the little Branagh is another sign of the king's might. An equally striking contrast is the apparent youth of Branagh's Henry as compared with the venerable bishops Canterbury and Ely. Despite the obvious superiority of these men in age and experience, when they are sent for, they come running to the entrance, futilely trying to appear more dignified. Branagh has also decided that their blessing should be delivered from their knees, in complete deference. Again, he shows Henry's power through others' respect.

Henry's entrance is even more effective when contrasted with the two other entrances in this scene: first Canterbury's and Ely's and then the French ambassador's. The bishops shuffle into the hall, which is completely silent. One suspects that they are late. Bunched closely together and slumped slightly forward, their movements suggest guilt or shame. As they enter soon after Henry does, the difference between Henry's honorable, royal air and their guilty, conspiring one is pronounced.

The ambassador's entrance is less suspicious than that of the clergymen. He walks quickly yet stiffly, and one hears the sound of his shoes hitting the ground as he proceeds. In the surrounding silence, the sound of the shoes is almost hollow, especially with the echo produced by the size of the hall. We sense the smallness of the ambassador compared with his surroundings. It is significant that while the entrances of both Henry and the ambassador are marked by rhythmic beats in time with their steps, in Henry's case these beats come from drums, while in the ambassador's case they come from his shoes hitting the ground. Henry's royalty and power, suggested by the drums, are highlighted by the ambassador's common status and lack of any special audio entourage.

Another comment on the effects of the exchange that follows:

In the exchange between Henry and the ambassador, Branagh tells the audience things about Henry's past which are not stated outright in Shakespeare's text. When the ambassador says, "You savor too much of your youth" (I. ii. 251), Exeter, the king's uncle, gives a quick glance at the king to see his reaction. He opens his mouth to protest, but decides to keep it closed. Slowly, the audience sees close-ups of about five members of Henry's court, and each has a tense expression of worry on his face. The audience can tell by the reaction of the court, and especially Henry's uncle, the man who knows the most about him, that Henry's youth is something not to be discussed. Branagh succeeds in including references to Henry IV, Part 1 *without using words or flashbacks.*

Finally, another student on the blocking of Henry's exit:

As Henry leaves the throne and marches off to prepare for war, it is important to note that Ely and Canterbury are, not accidentally, standing beside him and put on his cloak. In many ways, they are dressing him for war. One would expect a servant to put on the king's cloak, but the symbolism of the two bishops sending the king off to fight is effective. As Henry leaves the throne room to prepare for his voyage to France, he is followed by his entire court, marching in solidarity with him. The last people to leave the room are the two bishops, who, walking side by side, grin at each other as the scene ends and we see an empty throne behind them. They have won the day.

The group essay was a kind of celebration. Sections of every paper, and in some cases whole essays, were among the most imaginative things students had written all term. The class saw that. They listened attentively to the excerpts, and, in some cases, applauded. What made the difference? This assignment assures that students write original criticism: They can't get away with reworked *Cliffs Notes*. And they are writing from a position of genuine authority. Most feel at home with the medium, and, because it is the first production of Shakespeare for many, they are not hampered by preconceptions. They can look at both play and film with fresh eyes.

They also have a chance to double-check a reaction—to review the tape to confirm what they thought they saw or heard. A live production, while having more immediacy, does not allow students this replay, nor does it let them freeze the action or take extensive notes. Comparing a scene from both a videotape and a live production, though, can provide a useful variation on this assignment. Another possible variation is to compare scenes from two films—for example, the 1945 Olivier film that Branagh was both paying tribute to and positing his version against; the BBC or the Orson Welles *Macbeth* with the more radical Trevor Nunn-Royal Shakespeare Company production; Olivier's and Derek Jacobi's or Mel Gibson's *Hamlet*; or the tape from the *Playing Shakespeare* series on which Royal Shakespeare Company director John Barton talks with and directs two actors who played Shylock in successive RSC productions of *The Merchant of Venice*. Whether students are comparing two productions or writing about only one, I try to combat any tendency to leap to judgment, either dismissive or laudatory. Students cannot simply praise or reject a production. They must describe it in detail, and try to divine the reasons that the director has made a particular choice, even if they do not like the effects it creates.

No matter what the play, I have never given this assignment without learning something from my students, about the production, the play, or both. Besides giving the students confidence in their ability to understand Shakespeare, critiquing a scene teaches them a principle that is crucial to appreciating all drama: A speech, a scene, a play can be read in more than one way. The written text may be a stable entity, but its performance is a fluid process. Much of the pleasure of theater lies in the ways an imaginative director gives it meaningful shape.

Chapter 12

The Student as Director:
Antony and Cleopatra

By comparing different productions, including the scenes that they themselves have staged, students come to realize that there is no one "correct" interpretation of a Shakespearean text. This assignment puts each student in the role of director. The aim is for the student to describe how she or he would direct a key episode in a play that we have studied. For example, how does the student envision the opening and closing moments of the play, before the first or after the last word has been spoken? The opening music, the first actor to appear, the nature of the set, the period of the costumes should all reflect the overall impression that the director wants to create. Shakespeare is silent about how he staged those moments: The promptbooks that might hint at his intentions probably perished in the fire that destroyed the Globe. Are the witches in *Macbeth* to be played as old women? Androgynous beings? Are they malevolent or afflicted? Will they walk onto the stage, rise through a trap door, materialize one at a time?

Professor Miriam Gilbert asked us teachers at her NEH Summer Seminar to describe what we would have the audience see and hear at the beginning of *Twelfth Night*. A song by Feste; the sounds of a tempest at sea; Olivia, in mourning garb, leading a band of loyal followers; Orsino languidly gazing into a mirror or picking petals from a rose? And where and when did we set Illyria? On a Greek island, as in the 1987 Royal Shakespeare Company production? An Elizabethan court? An Edwardian nobleman's palace? A modern jet-setter's palazzo, complete with Saturday morning cartoons for Sir Toby Belch and Sir Andrew Aguecheek to watch and a private helicopter in which the Duke could arrive at Olivia's mansion, as in the 1990 American Repertory Theater production? What were the implications and the effects of our choices on the tone and characterization of *Twelfth Night*?

I have asked students to "direct" the end of a play—for example, the final moments of *The Merchant of Venice*, after Gratiano's last wry couplet about "keeping safe Nerissa's ring." The emphasis of his words is on the Belmont couples and the bawdry—the romantic-comic plot. But Antonio, the rescued but lonely merchant, and Jessica, the disloyal daughter, are present, too. And in the background, hovering like a shadow over the lovers' happiness, is the broken figure of Shylock. The threats to the comic resolution—social, religious, and emotional—are lurking just under the idyllic surface. Will Jessica and Lorenzo be happy? Will Antonio find an emotional attachment to equal his lost love for Bassanio? Will Portia and Nerissa find their new husbands sufficient matches for their ideals and wits? Will Shylock recover? Is there any possibility of a reconciliation with Jessica? Shakespeare's only stage direction is "Exeunt"—the Latin plural of "Exit." Every director of this controversial play has to suggest answers to such troubling questions, the student no less than the professional.

For younger or less able students, this assignment works better as either a live sculpture (see Chapter 5) or a sketch: Either stage or draw the final moments of the play. If we're doing the sketch option, all of us draw the stage and the figures on it, either in class or at home. When all the sketches are done, we hold them up and compare impressions: Is Jessica looking lovingly at Lorenzo or standing apart from the other couples? How are Portia and Bassanio distinguished from Nerissa and Gratiano? Is some reminder of Shylock present, in a thought balloon over Jessica's head or a sorrowful figure in the clouds? Is the setting outside on a moonlit night or within Portia's wealthy hall? Are the costumes Elizabethan or modern? After we have compared the different conceptions, and complimented the most inventive artists, we group the drawings by period or tone or number of characters and decorate a bulletin board with our artwork.

For older and more verbal students, the assignment has two parts: first, to write a description of their choices in blocking, casting, costuming, lighting, and set. Second, to justify those choices by explaining what they are meant to suggest about the scene's meaning. A variation on the before-or-after-the-play episode is to focus on a climactic moment within the play—a scene of confrontation or courtship or death. I have used that idea for both papers and final exam questions. Here is the form it took for an in-class essay on *Antony and Cleopatra*:

In the final speech of the play, Caesar gives his former rivals an eloquent eulogy:

> *No grave on earth shall clip in it*
> *A pair so famous...*
>   *their story is*
> *No less in pity than his glory which*
> *Brought them to be lamented.*

What are the main elements of this tribute? You are directing a new production of the play. How would you stage the death of either Antony or Cleopatra to reflect Caesar's view? You may describe choices not only about blocking but also about casting, costuming, lighting, or set—any aspect of the scene that you feel is important. Justify your choices by explaining what they are meant to suggest about the characters, not only the principals but also anyone else who is present.

The assignment is not without pitfalls. Even very able students may misread the tone of a scene and write descriptions that are either inaccurate or irrelevant. For example, one student thought that the "glory" that Caesar was referring to was his own, so that he was scorning rather than praising Antony. Some read only the "pity" in the tribute and created scenes that ignored the "glory" of the pair's defiance of Rome and the fame of their love. Some students may miss a key detail—e.g., that Antony does not stab himself with a dagger but,

Roman fashion, falls on his own sword, or that Cleopatra does not don her own royal robes and crown but orders Iras and Charmian, ladies-in-waiting and loyal servants that they are, to adorn her for her final scene.

Melodrama is also a recurrent temptation. One student wanted Antony's tunic to be stained and dripping with gore, another to have the moment of his death signaled by "a giant hologram of a stern Caesar projected against the sky," with "the sky split open, unleashing sheets of black rain…, a giant bolt of lightning, and a deafening blast of thunder." Another writer envisioned several large asps crawling around the stage, leaving trails of slime and threatening the incoming Roman delegation. Another thought Caesar should deliver his eulogy kneeling before the throne of the dead queen, and one wanted Antony borne in on a bier to share the spotlight with Cleopatra in a final tableau. Each of those excesses would detract from the dignity of the characters or spoil the decorum of the scene, and thus violate the spirit of the emperor's eulogy.

On the day that I return the essays, I mention some of the more egregious flights of fancy—though not, of course their authors. I also ask the most inspired "directors" (often the same ones who have gotten carried away at other points) to share some of their insights, either by exchanging papers or by reading out loud. If the latter, as with the papers on the professional director's choices, I create a collective essay, bracketing the best sentence or paragraph from several papers and arranging them in roughly coherent order. Each of these excerpts, I tell the class, constitutes "A" work. The following samples are from a set of in-class essays written by a talented group of seniors.

Here is one student's introduction to the issues:

> *In his final speech, Caesar pays tribute to his former rivals, Antony and Cleopatra. He states that they are worthy of fame rather than infamy (as one would expect coming from a rival). Caesar also recognizes Antony's glory, without which their story would not have such cause to be "lamented" (V. ii. 361). In his death, Antony has regained his "honor," "courage," and "noble blood" (V. i. 22–26), even in the eyes of the Roman soldiers. Caesar, upon hearing of Antony's death, goes into a reverie of sympathy and nostalgia for his lost "brother," "friend and companion" (V. ii. 42–44). Cleopatra glorifies Antony as godlike. Her description to Dolabella gives the impression of Antony as somewhere between Atlas and Hercules. In order for Antony's death to provoke this response, and not one of shame, it must be staged carefully.*

Another student described the effect that Caesar's tone would have on the staging of Antony's death:

> *Since these words are the last the audience hears, they leave a significant impression, and therefore the point of view they reflect was one that Shakespeare obviously agreed with. This is evident in the death scenes of both Antony and Cleopatra but particularly in that of Antony. In reality, he has two death scenes, the first one where he attempts to kill himself and the second when he finally dies. In the first scene, Antony asks his servant Eros to kill him, a deal they seem to have worked out before. However, Eros cannot bear to kill his master, and thus turns the sword upon himself. Antony reacts by praising Eros as "thrice nobler" than himself and then attempts to kill himself, "attempts" being*

the key word here. This scene reflects what Caesar later says both in its pitifulness and its nobility. While it is noble of Antony to think of suicide rather than face "penetrative shame," this nobleness seems to diminish when he asks Eros to do the job for him and especially when Eros, a servant, and therefore under Antony in rank, kills himself instead.

A third writer envisioned the casting and blocking of Antony's exchange with his junior officer:

> *Antony's tall, strong physique almost dwarfs a fair-haired, shorter Eros. Eros's subservience is clear from his smaller build. Antony has broad shoulders and a handsome face. Eros is noticeably younger, with smooth, soft skin. Antony is clean-shaven but with evidence of a beard. His complexion is dark, though not as dark as Cleopatra's.*
>
> *The scene with Eros and Antony should be played downstage center. Antony braces himself for the stabbing by standing with arms outstretched and eyes closed. Eros readies himself and proclaims Antony "my dear master, my captain, and my emperor" (IV. xiv. 89–90). His last words include a tribute to his powerful master: "Farewell, great chief" (line 93). When he stabs himself, Eros falls at Antony's feet. Antony opens his eyes to find Eros like an offering in front of him.*

Another student provided a more elaborate description of how he would cast and light Antony's last moments:

> *When Antony asks Eros to kill him, he should try to appear stoic. He wishes to die honorably, without a lot of blood, or the scene could become ludicrous. Antony, who should be taller and more handsome than Eros, should turn away only his face but not his body as he prepares to be killed. In his heart, he may fear death, but his body is resolute. Eros, in killing himself, should do it quietly, so that the attention remains on Antony and his reaction. We feel the pity that Caesar mentions most strongly when Antony says, "Thrice nobler than myself!" (line 95). He should fall to his knees, then fall on his sword. We feel even more pity when none of the guards will help him as he lies on the ground and they leave him. The men who bear him should hold him high, like a king, to Cleopatra's tomb, where he has been told she remains in hiding. There is the danger that this will appear funny, if Antony wobbles or if there is a lot of blood, so it should be played down, to center the attention on the emotion, not the props.*

Half the class chose to describe Cleopatra's death scene. Several commented on the queen's appearance. One boy wrote:

> *On hearing of Antony's death, Caesar sadly proclaims "The breaking of so great a thing should make/A greater crack" (V. i. 14–15). But this line also applies to the suicide of the great Cleopatra. When staging her death, one needs to make a deep impression on the audience's mind and create a powerful image of the fall of such a great woman. The actress playing the queen must be tall, thin, and overpoweringly beautiful.*

Another writer provided a rationale for those choices:

> *Physical beauty is crucial in their relationship. Antony is as handsome as Cleopatra is beautiful. The intense sexual attraction is important for both of them. Their love for each other is most apparent when they are apart. All they think of is each other.*

A third writer described her conception of Cleopatra's beauty:

Cleopatra would be dark-skinned and have black hair; she should look like an Egyptian to be convincing because that would be a source of the disgust that Antony's friends feel toward his relationship with her. Philo comments scornfully that Antony "now bends" the "devotion" of his eyes "upon a tawny front." He is noting Cleopatra's skin color and saying that she is not right for Antony and is leading him on. Because of Cleopatra's reputation as a promiscuous "gypsy," she should be voluptuous. Her costume should enhance and reveal her strong penchant for love.

Cleopatra should look her best during her death scene. Her face should be heavily painted; she should be adorned with ornate turquoise and silver jewelry, and her dress should be low cut and short-sleeved. Before she dies, she tells Iras: "Give me my robe, put on my crown. I have/Immortal longings in me." She wants to be as beautiful and as noble as she can when she dies because she wants to reclaim as much as she can of her pride, which she has lost to Caesar. Cleopatra is fiercely proud of her position as queen and ruler of Egypt.

Another student would use lighting to create a somber mood:

The scene should begin well lit, with Cleopatra ordering Iras to get her "best attires." After receiving the snakes (which she should put at her feet), Cleopatra should put on her robes, her crown, and the pearl that Antony sent her from Rome, signifying her continuing devotion. Iras has proclaimed, "The bright day is done/And we are for the dark" (lines 193–94). As Cleopatra kisses Iras and Charmian goodbye, the stage should darken somewhat. When Cleopatra says, "I am fire and air" (line 288), there should be a glow from around the pyramid on the backdrop. When she applies the asps (center stage), she should fondle the pearl she is wearing and her eyes should slowly fill with tears (she should not be sobbing). There should be a spotlight on her when she does this.

A different "director" would emphasize the pathos of the queen's death:

Right before her death, she would be in front of her royal monument, probably on a throne of some sort set upon a raised area. This setting would symbolize the power and glory, of Cleopatra and of Egypt. The time of day would be dusk, when only a few of the sun's rays would be visible. The sun would be coming from the audience somewhere; thus, the remaining rays would strike Cleopatra and her surroundings, giving them a soft reddish glow. The red would be somewhat ominous, and the time of day would symbolize the end of past glory. Cleopatra would be sitting slumped on her throne—unregal—and perhaps getting up every now and then to pace. She would have expressions of both shock and sadness, and her clothing would be messed, stained with Antony's blood and dirt from his grave. The overall effect would be a pathetic one: that of a once noble and glorious queen sitting ruined amongst architectural wonders.

That reading, while striking in its visual effects, is not entirely consistent with Shakespeare's text: Cleopatra is inside her monument, hiding from Caesar's emissaries, so the scene—and the lighting—should be interior. More important, this rendering overemphasizes the "pity" of Caesar's eulogy at the cost of the "glory." The final example includes both:

To reflect Caesar's admiration of the lovers, Cleopatra's strength must be apparent. She must not fall when she dies or cry out or moan. Her death should seem a show of strength, the show of strength that Caesar perceives it is. I would propose that she die seated; that way she will not fall when she dies. If this seat is a throne, it is one more reminder of Cleopatra's royalty and importance, even faced with Caesar's triumph.

Also important in this scene is Cleopatra's isolation from those around her. "All's but naught," (IV. xv. 81) she says at Antony's death, and for her that is true. Without Antony, she feels no joy in life. When the clown comes in with the asp, she is further alienated from human company. His inane chatter annoys her, and she says "farewell" four times, hoping to be rid of him. Her last reach for a human touch is when she tries to kiss Iras goodbye, but Iras dies. "Have I the aspic in my lips?" (V. ii. 292) demands Cleopatra. To show this sense of isolation, I would construct a pyramid-like platform, made up of steps, on which to place the throne. The set would be almost completely in the dark except for a light glow on the throne. I would tell the actress playing Cleopatra not to face the clown at all during their scene, turning around only at the end to take the basket. When Iras enters, Cleopatra should be standing on the first step leading up to the throne. On the line "Give me my robe, put on my crown," she would still not turn, but merely reach out her arms so that Iras could put them on. Cleopatra would not turn until the line, "So, have you done?" (line 289), when she kisses (or starts to kiss) Charmian and Iras. She would turn back to the throne on "This proves me base... " (line 299), and from then on not look anywhere but out towards the audience.

Though Cleopatra is isolated from those around her, it is also important to realize what she hopes to attain by dying, besides revenge on Caesar. By dying, she hopes to meet her Antony once again, or as she calls him, "husband." The setting should also incorporate a sense of her marriage to Antony in the afterlife. To do this, I would place a throne next to hers on the platform so that she could sit on one and imagine Antony sitting on the other. The two thrones would be identical and elegantly bare so that this scene would suggest the marriage of the monarchs, bride and bridegroom in death.

Ideally, students emerge from this assignment with the conviction that their own impressions count, and that Shakespeare is rich and protean enough to let truth reside in the eye of the beholder. Like his Egyptian heroine, age cannot wither nor custom stale his infinite variety.

Chapter 13

Shakespeare's Language

All approaches to teaching Shakespeare must eventually confront the problem of Shakespearean English. For the Elizabethan audience, it was enough to hear the words—they were written to be spoken, and spoken very rapidly. The Prologue to *Romeo and Juliet* says that the play will occupy "the two hours' traffic of our stage." Most modern performances take at least three, and in versions that have been cut at that. But Shakespeare's audience was more used to listening than to reading, and what they were listening to was closer to their own idiom. For modern audiences, listeners and readers, the strangeness of the language can frighten and alienate. The vocabulary and syntax are often arcane, the exposition rapid, and the scenes crowded. The newcomer hears that this is not prose and not contemporary American and concludes that it must be inaccessible—and boring. Often students "read" a whole scene without taking in a thing, without distinguishing between tones, motives, styles, or even speakers: All the characters seem to sound alike, and that sound is a stilted monotone.

The Right Questions

What to do? For me, first of all, to give up the belief that my students—or I—have to know the meaning of every line in order to understand a play. That is an impossible goal given the ways that English has changed since Shakespeare's day and given, too, the garbled state of some passages. It is also an unnecessary goal: Most good modern editions have ample notes on obsolete words and obscure passages. The bigger issues of meaning, I have discovered, become clearer as students get more experienced and more confident. Most new readers must be prompted to decipher and compare, to ask the right questions: What is this character saying? How is he saying it? What does his way of speaking suggest about his mood, social position, intelligence, sense of humor, regard for others? Is he a Good Guy or a Bad Guy, a Prince or a Clown? Is she her own person or her father's daughter, a queen or a trull? Usually it does not occur to the novice to ask such questions: What is on the page seems as inevitable as it does enigmatic. Students have to be helped to envision the playwright working purposefully, making choices, as they do themselves when they write. They have to be made aware that, like all plays, Shakespeare's consist of voices. The reader must learn to hear them. Once students have been shown the kinds of questions that it is "all right" to ask, they can usually not only answer those but also begin to pose equally important ones of their own—to read actively.

Versification: Rhythm as Meaning

The other big issue for teachers and students dealing with Shakespeare's language is the playwright's versification. Shakespeare's plays are written in blank verse. What does that mean? "Blank verse" is unrhymed—hence, the "blank." But it is not free verse: It has a basic metrical pattern, iambic pentameter. That is, each unit, or foot, contains an iamb, an unaccented syllable (marked –) followed by an accented syllable (marked '), which is repeated five times to make the pentameter. (A line containing four iambic feet would be called iambic tetrameter, one with three, iambic trimeter, and so on.) So, the short answer is that blank verse is unrhymed iambic pentameter—a definition easy to memorize, but hard to understand. I try to make the concept clearer by giving some short examples of iambs: the phrase "to wit," the name "Macbeth," or the name of someone in the class—"Michelle," "Jerome." "Banquo" and "Hamlet," on the other hand, are not iambs because the accent is on the first rather than the second syllable. That metrical foot is called a trochee. In other words, I point out, the division into feet is by syllable rather than by word.

I then ask students to find and mark a line of blank verse in the play we are reading. For example, Gertrude's first line in Act IV of *Hamlet*: "Bestów / this pláce / on us / a lít / tle while." After writing it on the board, I ask what is happening at this point in the play. Gertrude has come to tell Claudius about Hamlet's mad outburst in her bedchamber, but first she must get rid of Rosencrantz and Guildenstern. In this line, she addresses them with a queenly composure that she certainly does not feel, and she keeps her tone and speech rhythm carefully even: The blank verse pattern is highly regular. But as soon as they have gone and she is alone with Claudius, the meter becomes wildly irregular: "Ah, mine / own lórd, / what have / I seén / to night!" The line begins with a stressed syllable, and several feet contain not one but two stresses.

What makes this *poetry*? my students often ask. If this line is so irregular, can't we just call it prose? A good question: Unrhymed iambic pentameter comes very close to the rhythm of everyday English speech, and in fact long passages in most of Shakespeare's plays *are* in prose. Famous examples are Hamlet's "What a noble piece of work is a man" and Shylock's "Hath not a Jew eyes?" in *The Merchant of Venice*. Both speeches, though lyrical and vivid, are written in prose. Blank verse is more regular, more controlled. The five-foot pattern repeats itself, with variations, in nearly every line. The repetitive rhythm made the job of memorizing lines easier for the Elizabethan actor, who often had to perform as many as five different plays in a single week. It is the verbal equivalent of a basic dance step or a melody.

Although my students may be surprised to discover that they have been reading poetry, they usually accept this concept quite readily. What they object to is the idea of variation:

many would prefer the simplicity of a black and white schema—verse or prose, and, if verse, unvarying meter. Why are there variations? they persist in asking. Are the changes accidental? Did Shakespeare just have lapses in inspiration? I explain that the variations serve to emphasize certain words and to avoid monotony. In the line above, for example, in which Gertrude addresses Claudius, the opening sigh and the extra stressed syllables—every foot but the last is a spondee, two stresses in a row, rather than an iamb—indicate the queen's distress. The editor added the exclamation point to emphasize the desperation in her voice.

I also ask students to invent two lines of regular blank verse. First, we chant the rhythm and beat it out together on the desk tops. Then I try writing my own two lines, along with the class. The results are likely to sound like this: "And why / must I / attempt / to write / this stuff? / You'd think / that read / ing Shake / speare was / enough." Oops—it rhymes. That's not blank enough. In an actual Elizabethan play, such a rhymed couplet would be most likely to come at the end of a scene, to cap it.

Some students may find themselves writing slightly irregular lines. One, for example, volunteered these: "The girl / Took up / her pen / and wrote / great thoughts / Of love / and life / and lunch / in lines / like these." Which, I asked, are the irregular feet? The second and last in line 1—both are spondees, double stresses. How does that variation in the rhythm contribute to meaning? The first spondee—"Took up"—suggests the action of seizing. It has vigor and lift. The second—"great thoughts"—emphasizes, ironically, the loftiness of the girl's aims. The writer admitted that she did not think, "Now I'm going to alter my meter to suggest a change in meaning," but when her inner ear heard those variations, her critical eye approved of them. A similar explanation can be applied not only to spondees and blank verse but also to all the common variations in regular meter.

The following are the most common substitutions for regular iambic feet. I alternate between asking students to invent their own examples and finding them in the plays.

- Catalexis, omitting an unaccented syllable, most often the initial one: "What / about / the test / I have / in math?" The effect is to emphasize the first word.

- The pyrrhic foot, two unaccented syllables in a row, as in the third foot of this line, to slow the pace: "He loved / to sing / on the / long road / to town."

- The feminine ending, an unaccented syllable at the end of the line, to create a sense of anticlimax: "He looked / into / the box / and turned / it o / ver."

- The substitution of a different metrical foot for the iamb; the most common substitutions are the trochee, as in the third foot of the following example, and the anapest, two unstressed syllables followed by one stressed, as in the final foot: "He loved / to sing / ballads / and dance / with his girl." The first substitution implies the enthusiasm of the singer, while the second slows the line to deemphasize the unaccented words and suggest a lilting dance rhythm.

The following example incorporates all the variations listed above:

Bŭt whát / hắd ā [trochee] / yóung ānd [trochee] / cárefrèe [spondee] / lắss [catalexis]
    Tō sáy / tō ā [pyrrhic foot] / súitōr [trochee] / sō múch / ēnāmoúred [feminine ending]?

The predominant meter is nevertheless iambic pentameter. The reader, as well as the poet, should feel its beat beneath the variations.

As students who try such exercises can imagine, Shakespeare, like the other playwrights of his day, almost certainly got the iambic pentameter going in his mind and then kept to it or varied it by instinct. His audience, used to listening, felt the effect of that predominant beat and of the variations from it, just as a modern spectator hears a change in tone or pitch. Perfectly regular verse, such as we find in greeting cards, nursery rhymes, and comic scenes, is monotonous. The plays popular in Shakespeare's own youth were written in such a sing-song meter, and often in rhymed couplets as well. "The Murder of Gonzago," the play within the play of *Hamlet*, is a good example of this old-fashioned style. Here are the Player Queen's opening lines:

So many journeys may the sun and moon
Make us again count o'er ere love be done!
But woe is me! You are so sick of late,
So far from cheer and from your former state,
That I distrust you. Yet, though I distrust,
Discomfort you, my lord, it nothing must;
For women's fear and love hold quantity,
In neither aught, or in extremity.
                    (III. ii. 152–59)

The regularity of the meter, the rhyme, the end-stopped lines, and the antithesis of the ideas create a sententious, artificial tone. This verse is dry, rigid, lifeless.

There is a running argument about whether Shakespeare wrote or simply quoted from "The Murder of Gonzago." In either case, the sample of the old drama that he included in his masterpiece shows how flexible his own use of dramatic poetry had become. He could create the illusion that his spectators were overhearing actual conversation. Modern audiences, too, can "believe" such lines as "Well, good night," and "Now, mother, what's the matter?" At the same time, by formalizing the dialogue through writing it in verse, Shakespeare gave his drama structure and rhythm, and elevated the tone. It is more important to me that my students understand those concepts than that they master the intricacies of scansion. I let the blank verse question come up in the natural course of discussion, and I do not cover it in equal depth every semester. What I want young readers to gain is an appreciation of Shakespeare's accomplishment as a dramatic poet, of how he, like all great writers, made his style the perfect vehicle for his content.

Chapter 14

Shakespeare's Theater

In Shakespeare's day, plays were performed under conditions strikingly different from those of the modern theater. I am always looking for ways to bring to life an era and an architecture foreign to most of my students. I have found that even the pen and ink sketch inside the cover of the Pelican edition helps: At least students can see the open-roofed amphitheater, the two-gabled area over the stage, and the flag announcing the start of a performance. But what I have often wished for is one big visual aid—not slides or postcards or pictures in a textbook but a movie, say, of Rafe the shoemaker's apprentice attending a performance at the Globe.

The film would be similar to Sir Laurence Olivier's opening scene of *Henry V*, which is a reenactment of an Elizabethan performance, boy actors and all. But while that short sequence is confined to the interior of the Globe, mine would show the audience and the scene outside the theater as well. It would open with Rafe, an apprentice of about fourteen, at work in the shoemaker's shop. As he stitches a piece of leather, he listens to the periodic groaning of his master's wife, followed by the clucking and shushing of the midwife. Rafe's mistress is in the process of bearing her tenth child, three of whom have survived. The master has gone off on some business in the City, and Rafe is uncharacteristically alone in the dark little shop. He listens once more, sets down his work, and steals out the door.

Outside, he looks back over his shoulder, peers through the small window, and nods. It is an overcast afternoon, one-thirty by the tower clock. He smiles and hurries through the narrow streets, avoiding the side of the pavement closest to the reeking gutter. This is Elizabethan London. The streets are cobbled, the buildings timbered, the people boisterous. Upper-story windows open and women lean far out to empty chamber pots into the gutter; tradesmen pass, hawking cloth and meat pies and vegetables, dirty children play on the doorsteps. Several people, like Rafe, are making their way toward London Bridge, which connects the City with the southern suburbs. There, safely outside the jurisdiction of the puritanical London aldermen, the purveyors of the main forms of entertainment—theaters, bear- and bull-baiting arenas, and bawdy houses—run their profitable businesses. It is a Renaissance Times Square.

Rafe follows the crowd across the great bridge, pausing to stare at the severed heads of traitors displayed on its posts. He stops at mid-span to watch the heavy traffic below on the

Thames. In the distance, he sees a boatload of languid figures, who, having paid a waterman the penny fare, are being rowed in comfort across the river. Rafe shrugs, jingles the long-saved tuppence in his pocket, and presses on. Rain is beginning to fall and the Bankside is already muddy. A boy shouts something in his face and pushes a playbill into his hand. Rafe frowns at the paper, turns it sideways, shakes his head. He shoves it inside his leather jerkin and searches the scattered rooftops of Southwark. There it is—a black flag! The Globe is doing a tragedy this afternoon. He recalls his friend Dick's description of the duel he saw on the Globe stage the month before—real blood, Dick claimed, spurting straight out of the bad duke's heart, though someone said it was only vinegar in a pig's bladder. There was a ghost in the play, too, coming up through the floor of the stage in a cloud of mist, and a beautiful queen in real velvet and satin—even if she was one of the boys in the company—and a clown who danced the leapingest jig—oh, and thunder in the heavens, with real-looking lightning shot from a cannon, and a royal banquet right on stage. These visions of splendor have overwhelmed Rafe. He has stopped to lean against a large oak and let them wash over him, his expression a blissful grin.

The grin turns to alarm when he hears the blast of a trumpet from the turret where the flag is mounted: The play is about to begin. Rafe runs past the last carriages crowding the entrance, ducks into the door with the emblem of Hercules bearing his load—the globe—on his shoulders, and pays a penny to the member of the Globe company stationed there. He considers paying his other penny to mount the stairs to the first tier, but spends it instead on a bottle of ale that one of the vendors is proffering. He pulls a chunk of dark bread from under his shirt, sips his ale, and looks around in rapt satisfaction.

The theater is octagon-shaped. There are three tiers where spectators stand or, for up to six pennies, sit, as well as the big open space surrounding the stage where Rafe and the other penny customers stand. Since their place is on the ground, they are called, with Elizabethan directness, groundlings. Among them are former soldiers, apprentices from all the major guilds, and prostitutes and pickpockets already beginning to ply their trades. Rafe takes care not to stand too close to his fellow groundlings, who keep milling around and pushing toward the stage. The air is heavy with the combined stench of garlic and beery breath and sweat. Rafe lifts his sights to the higher-paying customers leaning forward over the balcony railings. What a crowd! Merchants and their wives and daughters, decked out in their finest; Inns of Court students; noblemen and their ladies, displaying their plumed and silken finery and their eloquence. They make as good a show as the players—in fact, some of them are seated on the stage itself, preening and interrupting the prologue with their jests.

The stage is a raised peninsula, jutting out into the sea of groundlings. It is unadorned by curtains and bare of scenery. Rafe stands on tiptoe and sees the trap door through which Dick has watched ghosts and devils emerge. Overhead, the blue, star-painted "heavens" form a canopy to protect the back area of the stage. Dick says that thrones and angels get lowered out of the heavens onto the main stage, and you can hardly see the ropes. Near the front of the stage stand two pillars, to support the heavens and to act as trees or hiding places or opposing cities, and at the rear is a small curtained enclosure, for bedchambers and studies. On either side of that recess is a door. The third trumpet call sounds from the musicians' box over the stage, and an actor emerges from one of the doors, dressed in black and carrying a placard.

It begins to sprinkle again, and Rafe has a moment to wish that the starry canopy covered the groundlings' yard as well as the stage, or that he could afford a seat in one of the upper galleries. Then the actor announces: "The Tragedy of Hamlet, Prince of Denmark. The ramparts of the royal palace at Elsinore." He bows and goes off through the same door, while from the other enters a man in full guard's armor, carrying a halberd. Rafe does not hear the young dandy seated on stage jeer at the actor's style of marching. He is intent on the action. "'E's not the prince then?" Rafe whispers to his nearest neighbor. "Not loikely," the man says loudly, giving Rafe a superior look. The sentinel paces back and forth, holding his weapon and looking tense. His back is turned when another soldier enters by the other door. "Who's there?" the new man demands. Rafe, like most people who get all their information through their ears, is a keen listener. He has only a second to be puzzled when the first guard shows that he, too, feels that the wrong man has asked the question: "Nay, answer *me*," he counters. Open-mouthed, Rafe is already oblivious to the daylight, the drops of rain plinking on his head, and the hand reaching deftly for his purse string.

We will leave him there, already planning to escape soon for another afternoon with the Lord Chamberlain's Men. Maybe some day the BBC will revive him or his nobler fellow-spectators in a short film designed to run before one of their Shakespeare Plays productions. Meanwhile, the play's the thing.